THE BEST OF TRADITIONAL
SCOTTISH COOKING

THE BEST OF TRADITIONAL
SCOTTISH COOKING

MORE THAN **60** CLASSIC STEP-BY-STEP RECIPES FROM THE VARIED REGIONS
OF SCOTLAND, ILLUSTRATED WITH OVER **250** PHOTOGRAPHS

CAROL WILSON AND CHRISTOPHER TROTTER

HERMES
HOUSE

This edition is published by Hermes House, an imprint of Anness Publishing Ltd, Hermes House, 88–89 Blackfriars Road, London SE1 8HA; tel. 020 7401 2077; fax 020 7633 9499

www.hermeshouse.com; www.annesspublishing.com

If you like the images in this book and would like to investigate using them for publishing, promotions or advertising, please visit our website www.practicalpictures.com for more information.

Publisher: Joanna Lorenz
Editors: Kate Eddison and Jennifer Mussett
Designer: Nigel Partridge
Photographer: Craig Robertson
Styling: Emma MacIntosh (food) and Helen Trent (props)
Proofreading Manager: Lindsay Zamponi
Production Controller: Christine Ni

ETHICAL TRADING POLICY
At Anness Publishing we believe that business should be conducted in an ethical and ecologically sustainable way, with respect for the environment and a proper regard to the replacement of the natural resources we employ.
As a publisher, we use a lot of wood pulp in high-quality paper for printing, and that wood commonly comes from spruce trees. We are therefore currently growing more than 750,000 trees in three Scottish forest plantations: Berrymoss (130 hectares/320 acres), West Touxhill (125 hectares/305 acres) and Deveron Forest (75 hectares/185 acres). The forests we manage contain more than 3.5 times the number of trees employed each year in making paper for the books we manufacture.
Because of this ongoing ecological investment programme, you, as our customer, can have the pleasure and reassurance of knowing that a tree is being cultivated on your behalf to naturally replace the materials used to make the book you are holding.
Our forestry programme is run in accordance with the UK Woodland Assurance Scheme (UKWAS) and will be certified by the internationally recognized Forest Stewardship Council (FSC). The FSC is a non-government organization dedicated to promoting responsible management of the world's forests. Certification ensures forests are managed in an environmentally sustainable and socially responsible way. For further information about this scheme, go to www.annesspublishing.com/trees
© Anness Publishing Ltd 2010

Previously published as part of a larger volume, Scottish Heritage Food and Cooking

PUBLISHER'S NOTE
Although the advice and information in this book are believed to be accurate and true at the time of going to press, neither the authors nor the publisher can accept any legal responsibility or liability for any errors or omissions that may be made nor for any inaccuracies nor for any loss, harm or injury that comes about from following instructions or advice in this book.

NOTES
Bracketed terms are intended for American readers.

For all recipes, quantities are given in both metric and imperial measures and, where appropriate, in standard cups and spoons. Follow one set of measures, but not a mixture, because they are not interchangeable.

Standard spoon and cup measures are level. 1 tsp = 5ml, 1 tbsp = 15ml, 1 cup = 250ml/8fl oz.

Australian standard tablespoons are 20ml. Australian readers should use 3 tsp in place of 1 tbsp for measuring small quantities.

American pints are 16fl oz/2 cups. American readers should use 20fl oz/2.5 cups in place of 1 pint when measuring liquids.

Electric oven temperatures in this book are for conventional ovens. When using a fan oven, the temperature will probably need to be reduced by about 10–20°C/20–40°F. Since ovens vary, you should check with your manufacturer's instruction book for guidance.

The nutritional analysis given for each recipe is calculated per portion (i.e. serving or item), unless otherwise stated. If the recipe gives a range, such as Serves 4–6, then the nutritional analysis will be for the smaller portion size, i.e. 6 servings. Measurements for sodium do not include salt added to taste.

Medium (US large) eggs are used unless otherwise stated.

Front cover shows Scotch Broth – for recipe, see page 29.

PICTURE CREDITS
All photographs are by Craig Robertson except: p7t Scottish Viewpoint, p7b, p16t and 17b Balvenie Distillery, p10b iStockphoto.

Contents

Introduction

Scotland's magnificent culinary heritage has a long and illustrious history. The heather-clad moors and dense forests that covered much of the land ensured a plentiful supply of game; the seas, rivers and lochs teemed with fish; beef, dairy cattle and sheep thrived in pastures; wild fruits, berries and aromatic herbs were gathered from fields and hedgerows; while the cold, wet climate proved ideal for oats and barley.

Below Scotland can be divided into three distinct areas: the rugged Highlands that dominate the northern half of the country, the bustling towns and cities of the Lowlands, and the remote, dramatic Islands that lie to the north and west.

The flavours of Scottish cuisine to this day reflect the rugged, hardy landscape. The wild mushrooms and berries complement the rich game meats, such as venison, wild boar and grouse. The smokehouses add a sumptuous taste to salmon, trout and haddock, and have resulted in local delicacies, such as Arbroath smokies and kippers.

Scottish cuisine has undergone a major progression during the past few decades, integrating new ingredients and concepts into the traditional fare. There has been an explosion of excellent restaurants offering superb dishes using local ingredients. Cottage and artisan industries have produced a wealth of speciality foods, such as jams, cheeses and breads.

A turbulent history

Scottish cuisine has been shaped not only by geography and climate but also by various social, cultural and political events. Its development was closely interwoven with the country's turbulent history – the threads producing a rich tapestry of flavours and traditions.

Over the centuries foreign invaders and settlers, particularly those from Scandinavia, had a powerful influence on Scotland's developing cuisine. The earliest impact was from the Vikings, whose lasting contribution was to teach the Scots how to make use of the rich wealth of the seas. Trade with overseas markets through Scotland's busy ports introduced new ingredients such as spices, sugar, dried fruits and wines to the Scottish kitchen. Politics too had a major role: the Auld Alliance with France, intended to curb the dynastic ambitions of English monarchs, had a great and lasting effect on the national gastronomy. All these influences brought new foods, cooking methods, ideas and skills, which over time became part of Scottish culture. Exposure to such influences occurred throughout the country's history to result in a rich and colourful cuisine based on high-quality Scottish produce.

A harsh landscape

Scotland is well known for its dramatic mountains, lochs and beautiful scenery. The geographical differences have also had a major role in shaping Scotland's cuisine and have resulted in different regional specialities according to the particular landscape and climate. The austere, rugged grandeur of the Highlands is the natural habitat of game birds, deer, rabbits and hares. The lush fertile land of the rolling countryside of the Borders and Lowlands supports beef and dairy cattle, sheep and goats while fruit and

Right Fishing boats bring in excellent shellfish to Scottish villages and towns, such as Tobermory on the Isle of Mull.

berries thrive in the rich soils of Tayside and Fife. The islands, lochs and rivers are home to a flourishing fishing industry which exports fish and shellfish all over the world.

Traditional favourites

The Scots have always made the most of their natural resources and magnificent produce and are careful to preserve their time-honoured heritage dishes. Aberdeen Angus beef, Highland game, Tayside berries, salmon and other fish and shellfish and of course Scotch whisky are recognized as the finest in the world.

The old traditional favourites remain popular: haggis is still widely made and is often served with 'neeps and tatties' (turnips and potatoes). In addition to national foods, every region has its own unique specialities, such as Forfar

Below Scotland is famously one of the world's leading producers of quality whisky.

Bridies, Selkirk bannocks, Arbroath Smokies, Loch Fyne kippers, Orkney, Islay and Galloway cheeses, Dundee cake, Moffat toffee, Edinburgh rock and a host of other delicious and much-loved delicacies that have been enjoyed for generations.

New speciality foods

A new generation of innovative and talented chefs has led something of a revolution in Scotland's restaurants, creating imaginative menus using Scottish produce, featuring many new and exciting signature dishes. Old favourites are given a modern twist and appear on many menus alongside traditional dishes. Restaurants in Edinburgh and Glasgow in particular blend Mediterranean with contemporary Scottish cuisine, and modern establishments serve dishes that fuse Middle Eastern and Far Eastern dishes with natural Scottish ingredients and flavours.

Food producers have also developed over the last decades, focusing on speciality quality foods, such as smoked salmon and whisky marmalades. Organic and free-range produce is increasing in popularity, with many farmers' markets springing up to promote cottage industries.

Fruit and vegetables

Flourishing for centuries in Scotland's long cool summers and fertile soil, fruits and vegetables play a key role in the Scottish kitchen. Various berries thrive in the hedgerows and wild mushrooms are collected from the damp woods and grassy meadows. These wild treats, along with the vegetables of the kitchen gardens, add nourishment and flavour to many traditional Scottish dishes.

Fruits and berries

Wild strawberries and raspberries were once plentiful though are now more scarce. If you can get hold of them, they are much more flavoursome than cultivated berries.

In the past, wealthy people grew peaches in their gardens. In the 18th century, ovens behind garden walls or hollow walls with flues, heated by furnaces below the ground, allowed many exotic fruits to be grown. Cherries, apricots, blackcurrants, gooseberries, strawberries, raspberries, plums and blackberries were all enjoyed in summer.
Berries The traditional Scottish kitchen garden would have berry bushes, especially raspberries, the national favourite. Other types of berry found in Scotland include blackberries, known as brambles; tayberries, which are juicy

and sharp-tasting; mulberries, which make excellent jams; loganberries, which are used to flavour stews and drinks; strawberries, which can sometimes be found growing wild in hedgerows; elderberries, which are a tasty addition to game dishes; gooseberries, which make delicious pies and crumbles; rowanberries, which are added to sauces and relishes; and rose hips, which make excellent jellies for serving with game.

All berries are delicate and perishable so keep them in the refrigerator and eat them as fresh as possible. Farm shops offer very good value, as the berries are usually freshly picked. Look for firm, plump berries, but remember that very large berries often lack flavour. To enjoy them at their best, allow them to reach room temperature before eating. Don't wash them until just before eating. Rinse strawberries very gently and hull them after washing to avoid making them soggy – the hull acts as a plug.
Orchard fruits The Lowlands produce some wonderful orchard fruits, although the season is short. Apples of many varieties are grown for eating and use in jams, jellies, pies and crumbles. Pears are also abundant, making fabulous preserves, jellies and pie fillings when they ripen in the autumn. Plums grow well in the Lowlands and are a favourite in pies and crumbles, as well as with porridge (oatmeal). Peaches and cherries are also grown, though not widely.

Left You will often find a bush of raspberries growing in a cottage garden or hedgerow.

Right Mulberries can be eaten just as they are when ripe.

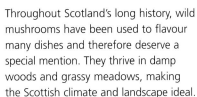

Wild Mushrooms

Throughout Scotland's long history, wild mushrooms have been used to flavour many dishes and therefore deserve a special mention. They thrive in damp woods and grassy meadows, making the Scottish climate and landscape ideal.

The flavour of wild mushrooms is far superior to cultivated mushrooms, with each variety having its own texture and taste. Wild mushrooms, both fresh and dried, are today easily available from specialist stores, grocers and markets. Do not pick wild mushrooms unless you are an expert or are accompanied by a mycologist. Some deadly poisonous mushrooms look very similar to edible varieties. If you add just one poisonous mushroom to a basket of edible varieties, your whole harvest must be disposed of.
Button (white) mushrooms sprout during the warm months, especially after rain. Commonly found, they impart a definite, faintly sweet taste when added to soups and stews. Larger varieties are called closed-cap mushrooms.
Common field (portabello) mushrooms are pink and white when young, with a delicate flavour. They turn almost black as they age, with a more pronounced taste.
Chanterelle mushrooms are a beautiful golden yellow with a fleshy cap, curly edge and the fragrance of apricots.
Field blewits or blue leg mushrooms are found in long grass or pastureland. They have a buff-coloured cap and the flesh is quite thick and chunky.

Above Leeks are a crucial ingredient in many Scottish soups and stews.

Morel mushrooms are one of the finest wild mushrooms and appear in orchards and forests in the spring. They have a honeycombed appearance and a meaty, nutty flavour, which is not lost when they are dried. Morels are never eaten raw, as they can cause stomach upsets.

Cep mushrooms, also known as penny buns, are highly prized with a nutty taste. Found in woodland, they can grow up to 1kg (2lb 2oz). Check for maggots.

St George's mushrooms are found in pastures. They have a meaty aroma, and can be fried, stewed or boiled.

Below Field blewits add a nutty flavour to soups and stews.

Puffballs range in diameter from less than 2.5cm/1in to more than 30cm/12in. When young and firm they are delicious sliced and fried or grilled (broiled). Take care when collecting them from the wild as they can closely resemble poisonous varieties.

Vegetables

Medieval French monks brought many hitherto unknown vegetable varieties, such as spinach, French (green) beans and cauliflower, to Scotland. Vegetable cultivation spread to the gardens of the nobility and by the 19th century Scottish gardeners were internationally famous.

Green vegetables are central to much Scottish cooking. They include dark green kale (or kail), which has the advantage of flourishing in Scotland's often harsh climate and is resistant to frost – in fact the flavour improves after a slight frost. Shred the leaves finely and cook for a few minutes in boiling salted water, as for cabbage, a staple item of the diet in Orkney and Shetland. Cabbage was preserved by being layered in barrels with fat, oats, salt and spices with a weight on top. It was then left to ferment, the result being similar to sauerkraut.

Leeks have a delicate onion flavour. Scottish leeks are distinct as they have almost as much green as white, so add a good colour to broths.

Wild leaves such as tender nettles can be eaten alone or in soups. Young nettle leaves can be cooked like spinach. Wild rocket grows prolifically in the Lowlands. It can be

Above Parsnips are a great favourite, either mashed or roasted.

added to stews or made into a salad. Wild garlic leaves grow in meadows and alongside pastures for a few weeks a year. They add a delicate, mild garlic flavour to dishes.

Root vegetables, particularly carrots, have a natural sweetness, which was used in cakes, puddings, pies, tarts and preserves when sugar was a costly luxury. Turnips were introduced into Scotland in the 18th century and they became the traditional accompaniment to haggis. Mashed turnips were commonly known as bashed neeps, or turnip purry (from the French purée) by the gentry. Potatoes were a staple food in Scotland by the 19th century. They form the basis of many old dishes. In general Scots prefer floury varieties such as Maris Piper, Golden Wonder and Kerr's Pinks. Mealy tatties (boiled potatoes) were cheap and filling, and were sold from carts in Scottish cities in the 19th century. Stovies is an old dish consisting of sliced potatoes cooked with onions. Cooked potatoes were mashed together with turnips or kale to make clapshot. Colcannon is cabbage, carrots, turnips and potatoes mashed with butter.

Fish and shellfish

Scotland is home to an ancient fishing tradition, its busy fishing ports ranging all along the coastline and the Islands. The natural harbours along the east coast have produced a thriving fishing industry. On the west coast, fishing developed after people lost their lands and began to seek sustenance from the sea. On the Islands, fishing has long since been a way of life. A plentiful supply of fish has always been part of the country's traditional heritage. Fish is often smoked or cured, as in the past, slow travel made the preservation of fish an economic necessity.

Preserving fish was achieved from the earliest times by wind drying (*blawn*) or sun drying (*rizzared* or *tiled*), pickling or smoking, according to the type of fish.

Entire families were involved in the business of fishing. Children collected and prepared bait and boys went to sea with their fathers when they were 14 years old. The women baited the lines, gutted, cleaned and cured or smoked the fish and also sold the catch – often walking some distance to the nearest town with heavy *creels* (baskets) on their backs.

Above *Salmon steaks contain the bone and are ideal for poaching, grilling (broiling) or adding to fish soups.*

Fresh fish

The fish enjoyed today are different from those eaten in the past. Sadly, some fish are less common now. On the other hand, fish farming has led to a greater availability of some fish.

Salmon is the fish most often associated with Scotland. There are two main types of salmon, Atlantic salmon from the sea and wild salmon from the rivers. There is now farmed salmon of various qualities. These all have different flavours, colours and textures. Wild salmon is the finest.

Herring used to be plentiful and cheap, but once caught they had to be eaten as fresh as possible. Tasty and nutritious, herrings can be coated with rolled oats and fried in oil for a few minutes or simply grilled (broiled).

Mackerel is caught abundantly around the coast and eaten as fresh as possible, simply pan-fried or grilled (broiled).

Haddock is now the most popular white fish in Scotland, often found in fish and chip shops. It is delicious baked or steamed as well as coated in breadcrumbs or batter and fried.

Cod is now an expensive fish, a result of overfishing in the Atlantic. It remains popular, often as a result of the many recipes and traditions surrounding it.

Left *Fishing boats are a common sight in many Scottish coastal towns.*

Above *Salmon fillets are the preferred cut for restaurants as they contain no bones and less fat.*

Sea bass is a flavourful fish with a fine soft texture, a favourite of the fish restaurants. Most is farmed these days as it is increasingly rare in the wild.

Monkfish used to be thrown off the fishing boats, but is now a prized fish.

Trout Rainbow trout is now enjoyed much more widely owing to new farms that have sprung up in the lochs and around the coastlines. Sea trout and river (brown) trout are rarely seen today.

Smoked Fish

In the days before refrigeration and fast transport, fish were smoked for preservation. Today fish are generally smoked for flavour. Haddock, mackerel, sprats and herring are smoked over oak, beech, hickory, cherry wood, Douglas fir or whisky barrel chippings, which all produce a magnificent flavour.

Smoked haddock is renowned in Scotland. Smoking haddock was a particular skill of the village of Findon (pronounced Finnan), south of Aberdeen, and it was from this village that the cure took its name. Pale golden Finnan haddock is famous for its delicate flavour throughout the world.

The original cures produced a hard, heavily smoked fish, but modern cures give a better flavour and texture. There are hot-smoked and cold-smoked cures, with regional variations.

Pales or Glasgow pales have a shorter brining and smoking time than Finnan haddock. Some are very lightly smoked and have only a slight smoky flavour and hint of colour. Smoked fillet, sometimes known as Aberdeen fillet, is a single fillet from a large haddock. The skin is left on to keep it together during the curing process. Golden cutlet is a fillet of haddock or whiting, with the skin removed, lightly brined and smoked.

Smoked herrings were freshly caught then dried over smoking seaweed and sprinkled with saltwater. Kippers are plump herring that have been split, cleaned and soaked in brine for a few minutes, then hot smoked. They can be grilled (broiled), baked or simmered in boiling water. An old way of cooking them was to place them in a jug of boiling water for 4–5 minutes.

Bloaters are whole herring that have been cured and lightly smoked, but not split or gutted. They have a delicate smoky flavour and remain silver in colour. They were popular in the 19th century.

Smoked salmon is the best-known type of Scottish smoked fish and is renowned worldwide for its quality.

Smoked trout is a favourite for making delicious pâtés and mousses. The best is brined, gutted then smoked over birch with a little peat for a smokier flavour.

Below Smoked halibut has a translucent white flesh and lovely delicate flavour.

Top-quality smoked trout is now made in a similar way to smoked salmon.

Smoked mackerel has a rich flavour and smooth texture. It can be eaten cold with a salad or made into a pâté.

Smoked halibut has a translucent flesh and delicate flavour. It is smoked and sliced in a similar way to smoked salmon.

Shellfish

The vast Scottish waters provide rich feeding grounds and yield some of the world's best shellfish.

Lobster is regarded as one of the tastiest shellfish and has a rich, intense flavour. Lobster is usually boiled but can also be grilled (broiled). The dark blue-green shell becomes scarlet when cooked.

Langoustines are a pale orange-pink with white striped claws, they are sold fresh or pre-boiled, and eaten hot or cold.

Crabs are caught in creels and are sold live or pre-boiled. There are two main types: the common brown crab or the

Below Native oysters are slow-growers and are considered the finest oysters. They are also the most expensive.

Above
Langoustines are now a speciality of many restaurants.

rarer shore variety. Their reddish-brown shells are tinged with purple and the claws are black.

Oysters were once so plentiful that they were a staple of the poor. Native oyster beds were overfished, became polluted and, by the middle of the 20th century, were almost wiped out. Oyster farming in the unpolluted sea lochs has brought about a revival. The Pacific oyster, often used for farming, is more elongated than the native oyster.

Scallops There are two types of scallops in Scotland – the Great scallop and the Queen scallop. The creamy white flesh is firm with a mild flavour. The orange coral is edible and has a rich flavour and smooth texture. Scallops need only a few minutes' cooking. They are also available still in their closed shells, when they are at their optimum freshness.

Mussels make a wonderful main dish or starter. They are commercially farmed, mainly along the west coast. They have less flavour and paler flesh than the wild orange-fleshed mussels. Horse mussels have a robust flavour. Mussels must have tightly closed shells; discard any that remain open when tapped (and any that stay closed once cooked).

Meat and game

From the lush pastures of the Lowlands to sheep-rearing in the bleak Highlands, Scotland's meats have the reputation for excellent flavour, high quality and natural rearing conditions. Scotland's wild open country has long been home to a large variety of game, which has always had a place on Scottish meal tables, particularly in the Highlands and on the Islands.

Meat

In the past, a soup or stew would spread a few smaller joints around a whole family, and the innards would be made into haggis, black puddings (blood sausage) and delicious pie fillings.

Beef from native breeds such as the shaggy, long-haired Highland cattle or the famous Aberdeen Angus – both of which tolerate the bleak, rugged terrain and harsh weather – has achieved international renown for its superb rich full flavour and succulent texture.

Beef needs hanging to develop the flavour and tenderize the meat. Good-quality beef is dark red with a marbling of creamy coloured fat – bright red, wet-looking meat indicates that it has not been hung for long enough.

Mutton and lamb have been favourites in Scotland for hundreds of years and in 19th-century Britain, Scottish mutton and lamb were renowned for their flavour and quality. Traditionally, every part of the animal was used – the shoulder and leg

Above Haggis is a traditional Scottish dish.

were braised or roasted; the blood was made into black pudding (blood sausage); the kidneys were fried; the heart, head and trotters were used in broth. Other parts went to make haggis.

The many breeds of sheep include Blackface sheep, a hardy breed that can withstand the harshest of winters, and Shetland sheep, a distinctive breed native to the Shetland Isles whose diet of seaweed and heather, together with the salt carried on the strong winds to their pastures, gives them a unique, slightly gamey flavour.

Mutton is still salted in the Hebrides, Orkney, Shetland and some parts of the Highlands. A small piece is sufficient to flavour a pot of soup or broth.

Haggis is a type of sausage, of which the outer cover is discarded and only the juicy inner meat is eaten. It is composed of mutton and lamb and their offal, highly spiced and bound together with oatmeal, and packed into a sheep's stomach ready for lengthy boiling. Today haggis is generally sold cooked, ready for further cooking and reheating.

Black pudding is another quintessential Scottish food. It is a blood sausage that is usually highly spiced. It is bought already poached and is then sliced and fried for breakfast or supper, or to slip into a sandwich for a tasty lunch.

Game

Scotland's wild open country has long been home to a large variety of game, which has always had a place on Scottish meal tables, particularly in the Highlands and on the Islands. Scottish game is unrivalled anywhere in the world.

Game is frequently cooked with the foods it lived on when alive. For example, rabbit is partnered with wild thyme, and grouse with rowanberries.

Venison from Scotland is considered to be the best in the world and is one of the glories of Scottish cuisine. Red deer live in the wild hills and are the most common. Roe deer live in forests and fallow deer inhabit forests and parks.

Farmed venison is less expensive than wild and the meat is more tender, with a delicate, less gamey flavour.

Most venison cuts should be cooked quickly and allowed to rest before serving, except shoulder and shin, which are better braised. The haunch, saddle or leg are

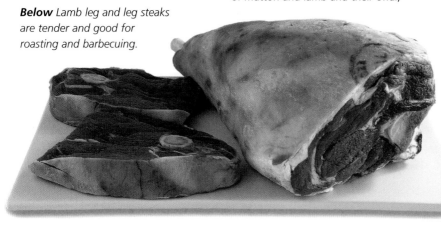

Below Lamb leg and leg steaks are tender and good for roasting and barbecuing.

best for roasting or for slicing into medallions. Chops from the ribs can be fried or grilled (broiled).

Wild boar is being produced by a few enterprising Scottish farmers – a recent development that is proving popular. It is a red meat with a slightly gamey taste. Noted for its leanness and flavour, it is sold fresh or processed into bacon and sausages.

Hare is a favourite catch in the Highlands. It is hung for seven to ten days and the blood is reserved to enrich and thicken the gravy. Hares are at their best from October to January.

Rabbit is best eaten fresh (although it can be hung), and wild rabbit has a stronger flavour. The meat tends to be dry so it should be well basted or cooked with liquid.

Wild duck are still available in Scotland, with mallards being the largest and the most common. Use them in the same way as ordinary duck, but add extra oil. The smaller wild ducks, such as the teal, widgeon, canvastail, gadwall, pochard and pintail, are highly prized. Young birds are generally more tender; older ones can be tough and need to be cooked long and slow in a stew or casserole.

Wild goose makes a tasty roast. The plump Canada goose is the largest and most commonly found, although the smaller greylag, pinkfoot and whitefront are also good.

Pheasant has a diet that does not include much heather as it does not frequent the high moorlands, so it has a relatively mild flavour. If eaten without hanging its flavour is similar to that of chicken. After hanging, the flesh develops a mild gamey taste.

Grouse has a unique flavour due to its diet of heather, blueberries, grasses and herbs from its home on the

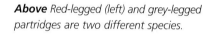

Above *Red-legged (left) and grey-legged partridges are two different species.*

Scottish moors. A native of Scotland, it is only found here and in the north of England. The flesh tends to be quite dry and, for this reason, it was originally cooked on a spit so that it basted itself as it turned.

Partridge is making a comeback after many years of decline, thanks to the efforts of gamekeepers and estate owners who have introduced the French red-legged partridge and the native grey partridge.

Woodcock has a wonderfully rich flavour and is still found in many gaming reserves. It is roasted with berries and root vegetables such as turnips and potatoes.

Pigeons are small and tasty, and are available all the year round, although each one provides only a small quantity of meat. Squab pigeons are the tender young pigeons that have a good flavour and texture. They are now farmed commercially and good-quality pigeons are available from game butchers.

Below *Wild rabbits proliferate in all parts of Scotland, providing excellent game meat.*

Below *The most common deer species in Scotland are the red deer and the roe deer.*

Dairy and baking

Dairy products traditionally played an important role in providing nutrients and protein in the diet. As a result, cheese, butter, milk and cream abound in the old recipes, as well as many new ones. Oats and barley are also highly nutritious, and play a major part of the Scottish diet, as do sustaining breads and luxuriously rich fruit cakes.

Dairy products and cheese

Much of Scottish cooking is based on the rich addition of creams, milks, butter and cheese.

Creams, milks and butter are added to many Scottish dishes, not only to creamy vegetables and mashed potatoes, but also to desserts and cakes. Cranachan is a delicious dessert traditionally made with fresh raspberries, oatmeal or porridge oats and fresh, thick cream. Many cakes and desserts are served with a dollop of fresh cream, such as tarts, fruit pies and crumbles. Cream and milk are favourites in drinks, especially with whisky, such as the sumptuous Highland coffee. Tasty butter has been made in Scotland for centuries. It is used in most dishes, adding a rich taste. Bread, bannocks and fruit cakes are all spread liberally with soft pats of fresh butter at teatime.

Below Oatcakes are delicious spread with butter and marmalade.

Below The wash for Bishop Kennedy includes a generous dash of whisky, giving a lovely tasty rind.

Cheeses In the past there were a great many Scottish cheeses, which were an important source of nourishment. Industrialization led to a decline in farmhouse cheese-making. However, there has been a resurgence of interest in traditional cheeses made by artisan cheese-makers across the country. These include crowdie, which is an ancient Highland cheese made from skimmed cow's milk. It is similar to cottage cheese, with a sharp, acidic flavour. It is unusual because it is half cooked. Fresh milk is left in a warm place to sour naturally, and then heated until it separates and curdles. The curds are hung up in a large square of muslin (cheesecloth) to drip.

Other Scottish cheeses include Caboc, Dunsyre Blue, Lanark Blue, Strathdon Blue, Cairnsmore, Scottish Cheddar, Drumloch, Isle of Mull, Tobermory, Tobermory Mornish, Orkney Farmhouse Cheese, Inverloch, Gigha Pear, Gigha Orange, St Andrews and Bishop Kennedy. The rind of Bishop Kennedy is washed in malt whisky to produce a distinctive orange-red crust. It has become popular in Scottish cooking.

Oats and barley

Scotland's cool climate is ideal for oats and barley. Rolled oats are used in oatcakes, bread, broth and of course porridge (oatmeal). Oatcakes are highly nutritious and, in the past, accompanied almost every meal.

Oats and oatmeal are used in a variety of foods and dishes, such as mealie pudding – a mixture of oats, onions, suet (chilled, grated shortening) and seasoning boiled in a cloth – and skirlie, which is oats, onions and suet, fried in a pan.

Soups and broths have an important historical role in Scotland's cuisine. *Brose* is an ancient dish, which was quick to make and nourishing. A labourer or shepherd would fill a leather or wooden hoggin (wallet or pouch) with ground oats, then add water from a nearby stream or brook. The hoggin was slung on his back and the continuous warmth and movement as he worked caused the mixture to thicken and ferment. The term *brose* has come to mean a variety of broths thickened with rolled oats.

Porridge became accepted throughout the British Empire as a breakfast dish and it was usual to add ale, porter or whisky. In Scotland it is customary to add salt – not sugar – to porridge, with cold milk or thin cream as an accompaniment.

Barley Bread made with barley was widely eaten throughout Scotland until the end of the 17th century, when oats became more popular as they kept longer. Although it is still a common thickener for broths, soups and sauces, much of the crop today is malted and used in the making of whisky.

Bere, an ancient variety of barley, has been grown and ground for food since the Stone Age. It was used by the whisky and beer industry until the 20th century. Bere is still cultivated in Orkney, where it is kiln-dried and stone-ground to produce beremeal for making bread and bannocks.

Bannocks and breads

Bannocks cooked on the bakestone and a variety of savoury and sweet breads have always been important in Scotland. **Bannocks** are thicker and softer than oatcakes, although similar in make-up. They are unique to Scotland and were originally unleavened in the days when every home had a bakestone.
Breads arrived with the advent of ovens in the 16th century. The Baijen Hole was an ancient and famous baker's store in Edinburgh. It was renowned for its rolls, called *soutar's clods*, which had a thick crust and were made from coarse wheat flour.

Wheat was grown in the fertile Lowlands, but bread made from wheat flour was eaten only by the wealthy,

Above Scottish morning rolls, or baps, are soft and slightly flattened.

right up until the early part of the 20th century. Regional speciality breads include buttery rowies from Aberdeen; floury baps (the origin of the name is unknown); fadge, which is a large flat loaf or cake, sometimes with dried fruit and nuts; the small round tod, or toddie; the wheat teabread known as whig; the large rye loaf called ankerstoek; and quick-and-easy buttermilk bread, which can be made with oats or wheat flour.

A wealth of cakes

The humble bannock had, by the 15th century, developed into a Scottish speciality, the rich fruity teabread. This was made by adding expensive dried fruits, honey, butter and spices to plain bread dough.
The Scottish fruitcake was baked in the bakehouses and kitchens of the wealthy, and served on important occasions. There are many Scottish recipes, including Dundee cake, which should be lighter and more crumbly than traditional fruit cake, and should have the characteristic topping of whole or split almonds.

Plum cakes were shaped by hand into rounds and wrapped in pastry (known as huff pastry), which protected the cake from burning during the long cooking process. The huff pastry was carefully cut off and discarded before the cake was served. The traditional Hogmanay cake is a rich, dark fruit cake encased in pastry, known as black bun. The pastry was discarded, but today the pastry is richer and is an essential part of the cake.
Sponge cakes became popular in the early 19th century. They were cheaper and less time-consuming to make than fruitcakes. High tea became an important meal, especially in the industrial towns.
Regional cakes were developed throughout Scotland, some of which went on to become world famous. Classic regional cakes include deer horns, Coburg cakes, Glamis cake, Montrose cakes, Scots snow cake, Sair heidies, Balmoral cake, Auld reekie plum cake, Portree plum cake, Kirrie loaf, Angus fruit cake and Caraway seed cake, which was a Scottish favourite and almost always featured at funerals.

Below Rich black bun is accompanied by a few whiskies at Hogmanay.

Scotch whisky

Scotland's gift to the world, Scotch whisky is unique and inimitable. It requires the Scottish climate, pure water and rich peat, not to mention hundreds of years of experience in the skilful art of distilling.

The origins of whisky are lost in the mists of time. The word itself is derived from the Gaelic *uisge beatha* – the water of life. As time passed, *uisge* became *usky*, then eventually whisky. The oldest reference to whisky dates back to 1494 when "8 bolls of malt to Friar John Cor wherewith to make aquavitae" were entered in the Scottish Exchequer Rolls.

Scotland's national drink was already well established by the 15th century and by the early 1500s had also become the favoured drink of royalty. During the 17th century the popularity of whisky grew steadily, especially in the Lowlands where many distilleries sprang up to meet the increasing demand. Highland distilleries were smaller than those of the south and supplied mainly local towns and villages.

In 1690 came the first mention of a famous whisky noted for its quality: Ferintosh, which was distilled by Forbes of Culloden. In 1784 the owner was bought out and Robert Burns immortalized the sad event:

Thee Ferintosh! O sadly lost!
Scotland laments frae coast to coast!

Cheap whisky became available in the 18th century, although it was rather nasty by all accounts, but good whisky, from Glenlivet for instance, was highly esteemed and expensive.

Whisky, especially malt whisky, is a versatile ingredient and its special taste imparts a distinctive yet subtle flavour to all kinds of dishes. Many of today's leading Scottish chefs have created marvellous recipes using whisky. Add a splash to a steaming bowl of those great stalwarts of Scottish cuisine, cock-a-leekie soup and Scotch broth; stir a couple of spoonfuls into a marinade for meat, game or poultry; soak dried fruits for a rich fruitcake in whisky, then feed the baked cake with whisky. Not only does whisky add a unique flavour, it also preserves and tenderizes; for instance fish and meat can be marinated in whisky before cooking. Do not be afraid to experiment by using

Left Laphroaig, made on Islay, is very peaty, and Whyte & Mackay is re-blended for a second period of maturation.

Above *This Speyside whisky distillery has a classic pagoda-style roof, which is typical of many traditional Scottish distilleries.*

different whiskies in a recipe; you will find that the taste of the whole dish is transformed.

Malt whisky

Aromatic, smooth and full of complex character, malt whisky is a drink of enormous variety and no two malts are the same. Single malts are the products of just one distillery and are the most highly prized. Vatted malts are a blend of malts from several distilleries within a particular region. Malt whiskies, with their complex flavours, vary in colour from palest straw to deep glowing amber and are more expensive than blended whiskies. This is partly due to their long maturation in casks that have previously contained sherry, port, rum or bourbon – which also augment their flavour and character as well as colour – for instance a fino sherry cask produces a light-coloured whisky, while an oloroso sherry cask results in a darker, strongly sherried whisky. Each region

Left *The Famous Grouse and Glenmorangie are both made in the northern Highlands.*

Lochnagar, produced close to Balmoral, is a typical example of a good East Highland malt.

The Lowlands produce malts which were the first whiskies to be drunk on a large scale, such as Rosebank. They have a fruity sweetness and a dry finish.

Campbeltown malts, from the Kintyre peninsula, are fully flavoured with a tang of salt, for example Springbank.

Islay produces dry, peaty and smoky malts. Some, such as Lavagulin, are powerful, while others, for example Bunnahabhain, are less so.

Above *Quality Scotch whisky should be enjoyed on its own or with ice.*

Blended whiskies

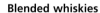

Blending malt and grain whiskies has created some excellent whiskies. Master blenders may combine more than 50 different malt and grain whiskies into a blended whisky. The normal ratio of grain to malt is 60:40. The percentage of malt used determines the quality, flavour, smoothness and character. Each whisky used in the blending process will usually have been matured for about five years, but there are also several longer-aged blended Scotch whiskies available.

Below *The casks are specially made from woods such as oak to impart a subtle flavour to the whisky.*

produces its own character, due to the individual and age-old traditions.

Speyside is the principal whisky-producing region and makes some of the world's greatest malts – Macallan, Glenfiddich and Glenlivet to name just three. Speyside malt whiskies are sweet and can be highly perfumed, with scents of roses, apples and lemonade.

The Central Highlands produce malt whiskies that are not so sweet. They tend to have a dry finish and a fine fragrance. Edradour is one example.

West Highland malts have a mild smokiness and a dryish finish, and include such fine whiskies as Talisker from the Isle of Skye.

East Highland malts are smooth and slightly sweet, with a hint of smokiness and a dryish finish. Royal

Breakfasts, soups and appetizers

A hearty Scottish breakfast is the ideal way to start the morning. Oats appear in many forms and smoked fish, such as smoked salmon and smoked haddock, is also popular. Other favourites include black pudding and rowies. Soups are a tradition in Scotland, as they make a healthy, nourishing dish for a whole family. Other appetizers are often based on the bounty of Scotland's coastline, as well as regional cheeses.

Rowies

These are the delicious traditional breakfast rolls served in Scottish homes, originally coming from Aberdeenshire, although they are made all over the country today and are very popular in tourist areas. They are eaten like a croissant, hot from the oven with butter or fresh cream and marmalades or jams and jellies.

Makes 16

7.5ml/1½ tsp dried yeast

15ml/1 tbsp soft light brown sugar

450ml/¾ pint/scant 2 cups warm water

450g/1lb/4 cups strong white bread flour

pinch of salt

225g/8oz/1 cup butter

115g/4oz/½ cup lard or white cooking fat

1 Mix the yeast with the sugar, dissolve in a little warm water taken from the measured amount then set aside in a warm place, lightly covered to allow some air to circulate.

2 Mix the flour in a large mixing bowl with the salt. When the yeast has bubbled up pour it into the flour with the rest of the water. Mix well to form a dough and leave in a warm place covered with a dish towel to rise until it has doubled in size, about 2 hours.

3 Cream the butter and lard or white cooking fat together in a small bowl and then divide the mixture into three portions. The mixture should be soft enough to spread easily but not warm enough to melt. If it is melting, refrigerate for 5–10 minutes.

4 When the dough has doubled in size, knock back (punch down) until it is the original size. Roll it out on a floured surface to a rectangle about 1cm/½in thick. Spread a third of the butter mixture over two-thirds of the dough.

5 Fold the ungreased third of the dough over on to the greased middle third, then the other greased third into the middle, thus giving three layers. Roll this back to the original rectangle size. Leave to rest in a cool place for 40 minutes then repeat the procedure, including the resting period, twice more, to use up the butter mixture.

6 Cut the dough into 16 squares. Shape into rough circles by folding the edges in all the way around and place on a baking sheet. Leave to rise, covered with a clean dry dish towel, for 45 minutes. Meanwhile preheat the oven to 200°C/400°F/Gas 6.

7 When the rowies have risen, bake in the oven for 15 minutes until golden brown and flaky.

Per portion Energy 296kcal/1233kJ; Protein 3g; Carbohydrate 25.4g, of which sugars 1.5g; Fat 21g, of which saturates 11.4g; Cholesterol 41mg; Calcium 47mg; Fibre 1g; Sodium 96mg.

Kedgeree

Of Indian origin, kedgeree came to Scotland via England and the landed gentry. It quickly became a popular dish using smoked fish for breakfast or high tea. This is a more manageable dish than the full Scottish breakfast when feeding several people, and it is often served in guesthouses and restaurants.

Serves 4–6

450g/1lb smoked haddock

300ml/½ pint/1¼ cups milk

175g/6oz/scant 1 cup long grain rice

pinch of grated nutmeg and cayenne pepper

50g/2oz/¼ cup butter

1 onion, peeled and finely chopped

2 hard-boiled eggs

salt and ground black pepper

chopped fresh parsley, to garnish

lemon wedges and wholemeal (whole-wheat) toast, to serve

1 Poach the haddock in the milk, made up with just enough water to cover the fish, for about 8 minutes, or until just cooked. Skin the haddock, remove all the bones and flake the flesh with a fork. Set aside.

2 Bring 600ml/1 pint/2½ cups water to the boil in a large pan. Add the rice, cover closely with a lid and cook over a low heat for about 25 minutes, or until all the water has been absorbed by the rice. Season with salt and a grinding of black pepper, and the nutmeg and cayenne pepper.

3 Meanwhile, heat 15g/½oz/1 tbsp butter in a pan and fry the onion until soft and transparent. Set aside. Roughly chop one of the hard-boiled eggs, and slice the other into neat wedges.

4 Stir the remaining butter into the rice and add the flaked haddock, onion and the chopped egg. Season to taste and heat the mixture through gently (this can be done on a serving dish in a low oven if more convenient).

5 To serve, pile up the kedgeree on a warmed dish, sprinkle generously with parsley and arrange the wedges of egg on top. Put the lemon wedges around the base and serve hot with the toast.

Variation Try using leftover cooked salmon, instead of the haddock.

Per portion Energy 399kcal/1668kJ; Protein 28.9g; Carbohydrate 38g, of which sugars 2.2g; Fat 14.6g, of which saturates 7.6g; Cholesterol 181mg; Calcium 62mg; Fibre 0.5g; Sodium 974mg.

Smoked haddock and bacon

This is a classic combination, very much associated with Scotland. The smokiness of the fish goes well with the rich flavour of the bacon – both are complemented by the creamy sauce.

Serves 4

25g/1oz/2 tbsp butter

4 undyed smoked haddock fillets

8 rashers (strips) lean back bacon

120ml/4floz/½ cup double (heavy) cream

ground black pepper

chopped fresh chives, to garnish

1 Preheat the grill (broiler) to medium. Over a gentle heat, melt the butter in a frying pan.

2 Add the haddock fillets, working in two batches if necessary, and cook gently, turning once, for about 3 minutes each side. When cooked, place in a large ovenproof dish and cover. Reserve the juices from the frying pan.

3 Grill (broil) the bacon, turning once, until just cooked through but not crispy. Leave the grill on.

4 Return the frying pan to the heat and pour in the cream and any reserved juices from the haddock. Bring to the boil then simmer briefly, stirring occasionally. Season to taste with ground black pepper.

5 Meanwhile place two bacon rashers over each haddock fillet and place the dish under the grill (broiler) briefly. Then pour over the hot creamy sauce, garnish with snipped fresh chives and serve immediately.

Variation
Instead of topping the smoked haddock with bacon, use wilted spinach for a healthier, tasty option. Thoroughly wash a good handful of spinach for each person. Then plunge it into boiling water for 3 minutes, drain well and lay across each fillet.

Per portion Energy 391kcal/1624kJ; Protein 28.8g; Carbohydrate 0.5g, of which sugars 0.5g; Fat 30.5g, of which saturates 16.5g; Cholesterol 119mg; Calcium 40mg; Fibre 0g; Sodium 1671mg.

Creamy scrambled eggs with smoked salmon

A special treat for weekend breakfasts, eggs served this way are popular in some of Scotland's best guesthouses and hotels and are a good alternative to the traditional fry-up.

Serves 1

3 eggs

15ml/1 tbsp single (light) cream or milk

knob (pat) of butter

1 slice of smoked salmon, chopped or whole, warmed

salt and ground black pepper

sprig of fresh parsley, to garnish

triangles of hot toast, to serve

1 Whisk the eggs in a bowl together with half the cream or milk, a generous grinding of black pepper and a little salt to taste if you like, remembering that the smoked salmon may be quite naturally salty.

2 Melt the butter in a pan then add the egg mixture and stir until nearly set. Add the rest of the cream, which prevents the eggs from overcooking.

3 Either stir in the chopped smoked salmon or serve the warmed slice alongside the egg. Serve immediately on warmed plates.

Variation

For creamy scrambled eggs with bacon and cheese, first cook 1 or 2 rashers (strips) of streaky (fatty) bacon per person in a non-stick frying pan until crispy. Then chop the bacon, add it to the egg mixture and scramble over a gentle heat as above. Just before it sets, add 25g/1oz/¼ cup grated hard cheese, such as Cheddar, and some freshly chopped herbs of your choice – basil or chives work well. Mix together quickly and serve immediately on hot buttered toast or freshly baked bread.

Per portion Energy 447kcal/1862kJ; Protein 37.3g; Carbohydrate 0.4g, of which sugars 0.4g; Fat 33.6g, of which saturates 13.1g; Cholesterol 734mg; Calcium 128mg; Fibre 0g; Sodium 1.37g.

Black pudding with potato and apple

This traditional blood sausage has come a long way from its once humble position in Scottish cooking. Made throughout Scotland and widely available, black pudding is now extremely popular, and even features on many a contemporary restaurant menu.

Serves 4

4 large potatoes, peeled

45ml/3 tbsp olive oil

8 slices of black pudding (blood sausage), such as Clonakilty

115g/4oz cultivated mushrooms, such as oyster or shiitake

2 eating apples, peeled, cored and cut into wedges

25ml/1½ tbsp sherry vinegar or wine vinegar

15g/½oz/1 tbsp butter

salt and ground black pepper

1 Grate the potatoes, putting them into a bowl of water as you grate them. Drain and squeeze out any moisture.

2 Heat 30ml/2 tbsp of the olive oil in a large non-stick frying pan, add the grated potatoes and season. Press the potatoes into the pan with your hands.

3 Cook the potatoes until browned, then turn over and cook the other side. When cooked, slide on to a warmed plate.

4 Heat the remaining oil and sauté the black pudding and mushrooms together for a few minutes. Remove from the pan and keep warm.

5 Add the apple wedges to the frying pan and gently sauté to colour them golden brown. Add the sherry or wine vinegar to the apples, and boil up the juices. Add the butter, stir with a wooden spatula until it has melted and season to taste with salt and ground black pepper.

6 Cut the potato cake into portion-sized wedges and divide among four warmed plates. Arrange the slices of black pudding and cooked mushrooms on the bed of potato cake, pour over the apples and the warm juices and serve immediately.

Per portion Energy 247kcal/1034kJ; Protein 4.2g; Carbohydrate 28.8g, of which sugars 5.4g; Fat 13.6g, of which saturates 4g; Cholesterol 13mg; Calcium 16mg; Fibre 2.4g; Sodium 132mg.

Lorn sausage with red onion relish

The Firth of Lorn, the region from which this dish originated, cuts through Argyll between the island of Mull and the mainland on the west coast of Scotland. Prepared simply in a loaf shape and chilled overnight, the sausage is then sliced before cooking.

Serves 4

900g/2lb minced (ground) beef

65g/2½oz/generous 1 cup stale white breadcrumbs

150g/5oz/scant 1 cup semolina

5ml/1 tsp salt

75ml/5 tbsp water

ground black pepper

Cranberry and Red Onion Relish, to serve

1 In a large mixing bowl, combine the beef, breadcrumbs, semolina and salt together thoroughly with a fork. Pour in the water, mix again and season to taste with salt and pepper. Pass the beef mixture through a coarse mincer (grinder) and set aside.

2 Carefully line a 1.3kg/3lb loaf tin (pan) with clear film (plastic wrap).

3 Spoon the sausage mixture into the tin, pressing it in firmly with the back of a wooden spoon. Even out the surface and fold the clear film over the top. Chill overnight.

4 When ready to cook, preheat the grill (broiler). Turn the sausage out of the tin on to a chopping board and cut into 1cm/½in slices. Grill (broil) each slice until cooked through, turning once. Alternatively, shallow-fry the sausage until cooked through, again turning once.

Cook's Tip
For the best results, use standard minced (ground) beef for these sausages rather than lean minced steak, as the higher fat content is needed to bind the ingredients together.

Per portion Energy 691kcal/2886kJ; Protein 50.1g; Carbohydrate 40.7g, of which sugars 0.4g; Fat 37.4g, of which saturates 15.6g; Cholesterol 135mg; Calcium 47mg; Fibre 1.1g; Sodium 299mg.

Spiced creamed parsnip soup with sherry

Parsnips are a naturally sweet vegetable and the modern addition of curry powder complements this perfectly, while a dash of sherry lifts the soup into the dinner-party realm. Try swirling some natural yogurt into this deeply flavoured dish when serving.

2 Cut the parsnips into even-sized pieces, add to the pan and coat with butter. Stir in the curry powder.

3 Pour in the sherry and cover with a cartouche (see Cook's Tip) and a lid. Cook over a low heat for 10 minutes or until the parsnips are softened, making sure they do not colour.

4 Add the stock and season to taste. Bring to the boil then simmer for about 15 minutes or until the parsnips are soft. Remove from the heat. Allow to cool for a while then purée in a blender.

5 When ready to serve, reheat the soup and check the seasoning. Add a swirl of natural (plain) yogurt, if you like.

Cook's Tip
A cartouche is a circle of greaseproof (waxed) paper that helps to keep in the moisture, so the vegetables cook in their own juices along with the sherry.

Serves 4

115g/4oz/½ cup butter

2 onions, sliced

1kg /2¼lb parsnips, peeled

10ml/2 tsp curry powder

30ml/2 tbsp medium sherry

1.2 litres/2 pints/5 cups chicken or vegetable stock

salt and ground black pepper

1 Melt the butter in a pan, add the onions and sweat gently without allowing them to colour.

Per portion Energy 437kcal/1820kJ; Protein 5.9g; Carbohydrate 39.5g, of which sugars 20.2g; Fat 28.7g, of which saturates 16.8g; Cholesterol 67mg; Calcium 134mg; Fibre 12.9g; Sodium 218mg.

Leek and potato soup

This is a hearty Scottish staple, forming everything from a warming lunch to a hot drink from a flask by the loch on a cold afternoon. The chopped vegetables produce a chunky soup. If you prefer a smooth texture, press the mixture through a sieve.

Serves 4

50g/2oz/¼ cup butter

2 leeks, washed and chopped

1 small onion, peeled and finely chopped

350g/12oz potatoes, peeled and chopped

900ml/1½ pints/3¾ cups chicken or vegetable stock

salt and ground black pepper

chopped fresh parsley, to garnish

2 Add the potatoes to the pan and cook for about 2–3 minutes, then add the stock and bring to the boil. Cover and simmer for 30–35 minutes.

3 Season to taste and remove the pan from the heat. Dice and stir in the remaining butter. Garnish with the chopped parsley and serve hot.

1 Heat 25g/1oz/2 tbsp of the butter in a large pan over a medium heat. Add the leeks and onion and cook gently, stirring occasionally, for about 7 minutes, until they are softened but not browned.

Cook's Tips
• Don't use a food processor to purée this soup as it can give the potatoes a gluey consistency. The potatoes should be left to crumble and disintegrate naturally as they boil, making the consistency of the soup thicker the longer you leave them.
• If you can, make your own chicken or vegetable stock by simmering bones and vegetables in water for 2 hours and straining the liquid.

Per portion Energy 179Kcal/747kJ; Protein 3.2g; Carbohydrate 17.9g, of which sugars 4g; Fat 11g, of which saturates 6.7g; Cholesterol 27mg; Calcium 32mg; Fibre 3g; Sodium 88mg.

Mussel and fennel bree

Bree is the Scots word for a soup or broth, most often associated with shellfish rather like a bisque or bouillabaisse. Mussels partner particularly well with the anise flavour of Pernod or Ricard. Try to get the native Scottish mussels that are smaller with a good flavour.

Serves 4

1kg/2¼lb fresh mussels

1 fennel bulb

120ml/4fl oz/½ cup dry white wine

1 leek, finely sliced

olive oil

25g/1oz/2 tbsp butter

splash of Pernod or Ricard

150ml/¼ pint/⅔ cup double (heavy) cream

25g/1oz fresh parsley, chopped

1 Clean the mussels thoroughly, removing any beards and scraping off any barnacles. Discard any that are broken or open.

2 Strip off the outer leaves of the fennel and roughly chop them. Set to one side. Then take the central core of the fennel and chop it very finely. Set it aside in a separate dish or bowl.

3 Place the roughly chopped fennel leaves, the mussels and the wine in a large pan, cover and cook gently until all the mussels open, about 5 minutes. Discard any that remain closed.

4 In a second pan sweat the leek and finely chopped core of the fennel gently in the oil and butter until soft.

5 Meanwhile remove the mussels from the first pan and either leave in the shell or remove. Set aside.

6 Strain the liquor on to the leek mixture and bring to the boil. Add a little water and the pastis, and simmer for a few minutes. Add the cream and parsley and bring back to the boil.

7 Place the cooked mussels in a serving tureen and pour over the soup. Serve with crusty bread for mopping up the juices.

Cook's Tip
Farmed or 'rope-grown' mussels are easier to clean. If you use mussels with lots of barnacles you will need to remove these first.

Per portion Energy 392kcal/1624kJ; Protein 13.4g; Carbohydrate 5.7g, of which sugars 3g; Fat 33g, of which saturates 16.9g; Cholesterol 105mg; Calcium 95mg; Fibre 2.8g; Sodium 297mg.

Scotch broth

Sustaining and warming, Scotch broth is custom-made for the chilly Scottish weather, and makes a delicious winter soup anywhere. Traditionally, a large pot of it is made and this is dipped into throughout the next few days, the flavour improving all the time.

Serves 6–8

1kg/2¼lb lean neck (US shoulder or breast) of lamb, cut into large, even-sized chunks

1.75 litres/3 pints/7½ cups cold water

1 large onion, chopped

50g/2oz/¼ cup pearl barley

bouquet garni

1 large carrot, chopped

1 turnip, chopped

3 leeks, chopped

1 small white cabbage, finely shredded

salt and ground black pepper

chopped fresh parsley, to garnish

1 Put the lamb and water in a large pan over a medium heat and gently bring to the boil. Skim off the scum with a spoon. Add the onion, pearl barley and bouquet garni, and stir in thoroughly.

2 Bring the soup back to the boil, then reduce the heat, partly cover the pan and simmer gently for a further 1 hour. Make sure that it does not boil too furiously or go dry.

3 Add the remaining vegetables to the pan and season with salt and ground black pepper. Bring to the boil, partly cover again and simmer for about 35 minutes, until the vegetables are tender.

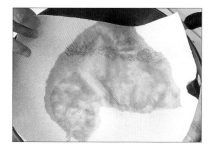

4 Remove the surplus fat from the top of the soup with a sheet of kitchen paper. Serve the soup hot, garnished with chopped parsley, with chunks of fresh bread.

Per portion Energy 387kcal/1619kJ; Protein 36.2g; Carbohydrate 17.7g, of which sugars 9.1g; Fat 19.5g, of which saturates 8.8g; Cholesterol 127mg; Calcium 86mg; Fibre 4.3g; Sodium 157mg.

Lanark Blue and walnut salad

Lanark Blue is a blue cheese made from ewe's milk near Biggar, south of Edinburgh. It is based on the French Roquefort but has a creamy texture and tangy flavour all its own. This is a delicious fresh-tasting first course but can be served without the figs as a cheese course.

Serves 4

mixed salad leaves

4 fresh figs

115g/4oz Lanark Blue, cut into small chunks

75g/3oz/¾ cup walnut halves

For the dressing

45ml/3 tbsp walnut oil

juice of 1 lemon

salt and ground black pepper

1 Mix all the dressing ingredients together in a bowl. Whisk briskly until thick and emulsified.

Cook's Tip
Look for dark green salad leaves, such as lamb's lettuce and rocket (arugula), and reds, such as lollo rosso, as well as some crunchy leaves, such as Little Gem (Bibb), to add interest.

Variation
The figs may be replaced with ripe nectarines or peaches if you prefer. Wash and cut in half, discard the stone, then cut each half into three or four slices. If the skin is tough, you may need to remove it.

2 Wash and dry the salad leaves then tear them gently into bitesize pieces. Place in a mixing bowl and toss with the dressing. Transfer to a large serving dish or divide among four individual plates, ensuring a good balance of colour and texture on each plate.

3 Cut the figs into quarters and add to the salad leaves.

4 Sprinkle the cheese over, crumbling it slightly. Then sprinkle over the walnuts, breaking them up roughly in your fingers as you go.

Per portion Energy 415kcal/1726kJ; Protein 10.6g; Carbohydrate 26.6g, of which sugars 26.4g; Fat 30.3g, of which saturates 7.3g; Cholesterol 22mg; Calcium 286mg; Fibre 4.5g; Sodium 383mg.

Grilled oysters with Highland heather honey

Heather honey is very fragrant, the pollen gathered by bees late in the season when the heather on the moors is in full flower. Beekeepers in Scotland will take their hives up to the hills once the spring and early summer blossoms are over, so the flavour is more intense.

Serves 4

1 bunch spring onions (scallions), washed

20ml/4 tsp heather honey

10ml/2 tsp soy sauce

16 fresh oysters

4 Place a large teaspoon of the honey and spring onion mixture on top of each oyster.

5 Place under the preheated grill until the mixture bubbles, which will take about 5 minutes. Take care when removing the oysters from the grill as the shells retain the heat. Make sure that you don't lose any of the sauce from inside the oyster shells.

6 Allow the oysters to cool slightly before serving with slices of bread to soak up the juices. Either tip them straight into your mouth or lift them out with a spoon or fork.

1 Preheat the grill (broiler) to medium. Chop the spring onions finely, removing any coarser outer leaves.

2 Place the heather honey and soy sauce in a bowl and mix. Then add the finely chopped spring onions and mix them in thoroughly.

3 Open the oysters with an oyster knife or a small, sharp knife, taking care to catch the liquid in a small bowl. Leave the oysters attached to one side of the shell. Strain the liquid to remove any pieces of broken shell, and set aside.

Per portion Energy 81kcal/343kJ; Protein 9.2g; Carbohydrate 9.1g, of which sugars 6.9g; Fat 1.2g, of which saturates 0.2g; Cholesterol 46mg; Calcium 121mg; Fibre 0.3g; Sodium 588mg.

Mussels with Musselburgh leeks

Musselburgh is a former fishing port near Edinburgh, famous for its oyster beds and its leeks – a short, stumpy variety with huge green tops and an excellent flavour.

Serves 4

1.3kg/3lb mussels

1 leek, cut into 5cm/2in lengths

50g/2oz/¼ cup butter

1 onion, finely chopped

pinch of saffron threads

150ml/¼ pint/⅔ cup dry white wine

1 bay leaf

sprig of fresh thyme

6 black peppercorns

100ml/3½fl oz/scant ½ cup double (heavy) cream

ground black pepper

chopped fresh parsley, to garnish

1 Scrub the mussels in plenty of cold water and discard any that are broken or remain open when tapped lightly against the work surface.

2 Remove the beard from each mussel by pulling hard towards the pointed tip of the mussel.

3 Use as small, sharp knife to scrape off any barnacles.

4 Wash the leek under cold running water. Discard any tough outer leaves.

5 Cut the leek into fine strips or batons.

6 Melt the butter in a heavy pan then sweat the onion gently until soft. Add the saffron threads and stir for a few minutes, then add the leek batons and allow to wilt slightly.

7 Add the mussels with the wine, herbs and peppercorns. Cover and steam over a medium heat until the mussel shells open, about 5 minutes. Discard any that remain closed.

8 Remove the lid from the pan and add the cream. Simmer rapidly to allow the sauce to thicken slightly. Remove the bay leaf and thyme, and stir well to mix the leek around.

9 Serve immediately in warmed bowls, with a grind or two of black pepper and garnished with lots of chopped fresh parsley. Provide hot, crusty bread for mopping up the sauce.

Per portion Energy 332kcal/1379kJ; Protein 17.6g; Carbohydrate 1.9g, of which sugars 1.6g; Fat 25.7g, of which saturates 15.2g; Cholesterol 100mg; Calcium 214mg; Fibre 0.2g; Sodium 288mg.

Smoked haddock pâté

Arbroath smokies are small haddock that are beheaded and gutted but not split before being salted and hot-smoked. You can also use kippers or any smoked fish for this recipe.

Serves 6

3 large Arbroath smokies, approximately 225g/8oz each

275g/10oz/1¼ cups soft cheese

3 eggs, beaten

30–45ml/2–3 tbsp lemon juice

ground black pepper

sprigs of chervil, to garnish

lettuce and lemon wedges, to serve

1 Preheat the oven to 160°C/325°F/Gas 3 and butter six ramekin dishes. Lay the smokies in a baking dish and heat them through in the oven for 10 minutes.

2 Remove the fish from the oven, carefully remove the skin and bones then flake the flesh into a bowl.

3 Mash the fish with a fork then work in the cheese, then the eggs. Add lemon juice and pepper to taste.

4 Divide the fish mixture among the ramekin dishes and place them in a large roasting pan. Pour hot water into the roasting pan to come halfway up the dishes. Bake in the oven for 30 minutes, until just set.

5 Leave to cool for 2–3 minutes, then run a sharp knife around the edge of each dish and carefully invert the pâté on to warmed plates. Garnish with chervil sprigs and serve with the lettuce leaves and lemon wedges.

Per portion Energy 206kcal/859kJ; Protein 25.3g; Carbohydrate 1.7g, of which sugars 0.1g; Fat 11g, of which saturates 5.8g; Cholesterol 153mg; Calcium 82mg; Fibre 0g; Sodium 940mg.

Haddock and smoked salmon terrine

This substantial terrine makes a superb dish for a summer buffet, accompanied by dill mayonnaise and served with a light, crisp salad.

Serves 10–12 as a first course, 6–8 as a main course

15ml/1 tbsp sunflower oil, for greasing

350g/12oz oak-smoked salmon

900g/2lb haddock fillets, skinned

2 eggs, lightly beaten

105ml/7 tbsp crème fraîche

30ml/2 tbsp drained capers

30ml/2 tbsp drained soft green or pink peppercorns

salt and ground white pepper

crème fraîche, peppercorns, fresh dill and rocket (arugula), to garnish

1 Preheat the oven to 200°C/400°F/ Gas 6. Grease a 1 litre/1¾ pint/4 cup loaf tin (pan) or terrine with the oil. Use half of the salmon to line the tin or terrine, letting some of the ends overhang the mould. Reserve the remaining smoked salmon.

Variation
Use any thick white fish fillets for this terrine – try halibut or Arctic bass. Cod is also good, although it is better to use a firm, chunky piece that will not crumble easily after being cooked. You could also use fresh salmon for a truly salmony flavour.

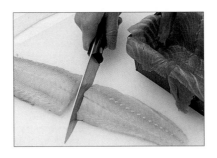

2 Cut two long slices of haddock the length of the tin or terrine and set them aside. Cut the remaining haddock into small pieces. Season all the haddock.

3 Combine the eggs, crème fraîche, capers and peppercorns in a bowl. Season, then stir in the small pieces of haddock. Spoon the mixture into the tin or terrine until one-third full. Smooth the surface with a spatula.

4 Wrap the reserved long haddock fillets in the reserved smoked salmon. Lay them on top of the fish mixture in the tin or terrine.

5 Fill the tin or terrine with the rest of the fish mixture, smooth over the surface and fold the overhanging pieces of smoked salmon over the top. Cover tightly with a double thickness of foil. Tap the terrine to settle the contents.

6 Stand the terrine in a roasting pan and pour in boiling water to come halfway up the sides. Place in the preheated oven and cook for 45 minutes–1 hour.

7 Take the terrine out of the roasting pan, but do not remove the foil cover. Place two or three large heavy tins on the foil to weight it and leave until cold. Chill in the refrigerator for 24 hours.

8 About 1 hour before serving, lift off the weights and remove the foil. Carefully invert the terrine on to a serving plate and lift off the terrine. Serve the terrine in thick slices with crème fraîche, peppercorns, fronds of dill and rocket leaves.

Per portion Energy 187kcal/785kJ; Protein 27.5g; Carbohydrate 0.3g, of which sugars 0.2g; Fat 8.5g, of which saturates 3.7g; Cholesterol 95mg; Calcium 31mg; Fibre 0g; Sodium 735mg.

Fish and shellfish

The sea, the loch and the river have always provided
the mainstay of the diet in the Highlands and Islands
of Scotland, where the rugged mountains provide
little in the way of food and nourishment. Salmon is
perhaps the king of Scottish fish, and the rivers are
renowned for the best in leaping fresh wild Scottish
salmon. Today there are some fishing villages on the
coasts and Islands where fishermen still bring in
the daily catch, including haddock, sea trout,
lobsters, crabs and prawns, although there has been
a decline in the industry due to overfishing.

Clam stovies

Clams are now harvested in the lochs, especially in Loch Fyne where some of the best Scottish clams are grown on ropes. Limpets or cockles can also be used if you can buy them fresh or collect them yourself along the seashore.

Serves 4

2.5 litres/4 pints/10 cups clams

potatoes (see step 3)

oil, for greasing

chopped fresh flat leaf parsley, to garnish

50g/2oz/¼ cup butter

salt and ground black pepper

1 Wash the clams and soak them overnight in fresh cold water. This will clean them out and get rid of any sand and other detritus.

2 Preheat the oven to 190°C/375°F/Gas 5. Put the clams into a large pan, cover with water and bring to the boil. Add a little salt then simmer until the shells open. Reserve the cooking liquor. Shell the clams, reserving a few whole.

3 Weigh the shelled clams. You will need three times their weight in unpeeled potatoes.

4 Peel and slice the potatoes thinly. Lightly oil the base and sides of a flameproof, ovenproof dish. Arrange a layer of potatoes in the base of the dish, add a layer of the clams and season with a little salt and ground black pepper. Repeat until the ingredients are all used, finishing with a layer of potatoes on top. Finally, season lightly.

5 Pour in some of the reserved cooking liquor to come about halfway up the dish. Dot the top with the butter then cover with foil. Bring to the boil on the stove over a medium-high heat, then bake in the preheated oven for 2 hours until the top is golden brown.

6 Serve hot, garnished with chopped fresh flat leaf parsley.

Per portion Energy 320kcal/1348kJ; Protein 17.3g; Carbohydrate 36.7g, of which sugars 3.3g; Fat 12.6g, of which saturates 7g; Cholesterol 57mg; Calcium 188mg; Fibre 2.9g; Sodium 262mg.

Queenies with smoked Ayrshire bacon

This recipe uses the classic combination of scallops with bacon, but this time using princess scallops – known locally as 'Queenies' – which are cooked with a flavoursome cured bacon known as smoked Ayrshire bacon.

Serves 4

6 rashers (strips) smoked Ayrshire bacon, cut into thin strips

5ml/1 tsp ground turmeric

28 princess scallops

1 sprig each of parsley and thyme

1 bay leaf

6 black peppercorns

150ml/¼ pint/⅔ cup dry white wine

75ml/2½ fl oz/⅓ cup double (heavy) cream

30ml/2 tbsp chopped fresh chives, to garnish

1 Using a pan with a close-fitting lid, fry the bacon in its own fat until well cooked and crisp. Remove the bacon.

2 Reduce the heat, stir the turmeric into the juices and cook for 1 2 minutes.

3 Add the scallops to the pan with the herbs and peppercorns. Carefully pour in the wine (it will steam) and then cover with the lid. The scallops will only take a few minutes to cook. Test them by removing a thick one and piercing with a sharp knife to see if they are soft. Once they are cooked, remove from the pan and keep warm.

4 Stir in the cream and increase the heat to allow the sauce to simmer. This should be a light sauce; if it becomes too thick then add a little water.

5 Serve the scallops in warmed bowls or on plates with the sauce ladled over. Sprinkle with the crisp bacon and garnish with chopped fresh chives.

Per portion Energy 353kcal/1476kJ; Protein 36.5g; Carbohydrate 4.8g, of which sugars 0.5g; Fat 18.4g, of which saturates 9.1g; Cholesterol 106mg; Calcium 51mg; Fibre 0g; Sodium 904mg.

East Neuk lobster with wholegrain mustard and cream

The East Neuk of Fife is the 'corner' of Fife on the east coast of Scotland, an area bounded by the sea almost all around. From Elie to St Andrews, there is a proliferation of fishing villages, which in their time provided the vast majority of jobs in the area. Today Pittenweem is the only real fishing port with its own fish and shellfish market.

Serves 2

1 lobster, approximately 500g/1¼lb

10ml/2 tsp butter

splash of whisky (grain not malt)

1 shallot or ½ onion, finely chopped

50g/2oz button (white) mushrooms

splash of white wine

175ml/6fl oz/¾ cup double (heavy) cream

5ml/1 tsp wholegrain mustard

10ml/2 tsp chopped fresh chervil and a little tarragon

60ml/4 tbsp breadcrumbs

50g/2oz/¼ cup butter, melted

salt and ground black pepper

1 Cook the lobster in boiling salted water for about 7 minutes then set aside to cool.

Cook's Tip
You can use a precooked lobster or prepared lobster meat for this recipe if you prefer.

2 Once cool, cut the lobster down the middle, top to bottom, and remove the intestines down the back.

3 Remove the meat from the tail, taking care not to let it break into pieces.

4 Cut the tail meat into slanted slices. Remove the meat from the claws, keeping it as whole as possible. Wash the two half-shells out and set aside.

5 Heat a frying pan over a low heat, add the butter and wait for it to bubble. Gently add the lobster meat and colour lightly (don't overcook or it will dry out). Pour in the whisky. If you have a gas hob, allow the flames to get inside the pan to briefly flame the pieces and burn off the alcohol; if the hob is electric, don't worry as it isn't vital. Remove the lobster meat.

6 Add the chopped shallot or onion and the mushrooms, and cook gently over a medium-low heat for a few minutes until soft and the onion or shallot is transparent. Add a little white wine, then the cream, and allow to simmer to reduce to a light coating texture. Then add the mustard and the chopped herbs and mix well. Season to taste with a little salt and freshly ground black pepper. Meanwhile preheat the grill (broiler) to high.

7 Place the two lobster half-shells on the grill pan. Distribute the lobster meat evenly throughout the two half-shells and spoon the sauce over. Sprinkle with breadcrumbs, drizzle with melted butter and brown under the preheated grill. Serve immediately.

Per portion Energy 812kcal/3357kJ; Protein 23.6g; Carbohydrate 12g, of which sugars 3.7g; Fat 74.9g, of which saturates 46g; Cholesterol 287mg; Calcium 127mg; Fibre 0.9g; Sodium 580mg.

Baked salmon with watercress sauce

The quintessential Scottish centrepiece, the whole baked salmon makes a stunning focal point for a buffet. Baking it in foil is easier than poaching and retains the melting quality. Decorating the fish with thin slices of cucumber adds to this Highland delight.

Serves 6–8

2–3kg/4½–6½lb salmon, cleaned, with head and tail left on

3–5 spring onions (scallions), thinly sliced

1 lemon, thinly sliced

1 cucumber, thinly sliced

salt and ground black pepper

sprigs of fresh dill, to garnish

lemon wedges, to serve

For the sauce

3 garlic cloves, chopped

200g/7oz watercress leaves, finely chopped

40g/1½oz/¾ cup finely chopped fresh tarragon

300g/11oz/1¼ cups mayonnaise

15–30ml/1–2 tbsp lemon juice

200g/7oz/scant 1 cup unsalted (sweet) butter

1 Preheat the oven to 180°C/350°F/Gas 4. Rinse the salmon and lay it on a large piece of foil. Stuff the fish with the slices of spring onions and lemon, then season the fish with salt and black pepper.

2 Loosely fold the foil around the fish and fold the edges over to seal. Bake in the preheated oven for about 1 hour.

3 Remove the fish from the oven and leave it to stand, still wrapped in the foil, for about 15 minutes. Then gently unwrap the foil parcel and set the salmon aside to cool.

4 When the fish has cooled, carefully lift it on to a large plate, still covered with lemon slices. Cover the fish tightly with clear film (plastic wrap) and chill for several hours in the refrigerator.

5 Remove the lemon slices from the top of the fish. Use a blunt knife to lift up the edge of the skin and carefully peel the skin away from the flesh, avoiding tearing the flesh. Pull out any fins at the same time. Carefully turn the salmon over and repeat on the other side. Leave the head on for serving, if you wish. Discard the skin.

Variation
If you prefer to poach the fish rather than baking it, you will need to use a fish kettle. Place the salmon on the rack in the kettle. Cover the salmon completely with cold water, place the lid over to cover, and slowly bring to a simmer. Cook for 5–10 minutes per 450g/1lb until tender.

6 To make the sauce, put the garlic, watercress, tarragon, mayonnaise and lemon juice in a food processor or bowl, and process or mix to combine.

7 Melt the butter then add to the watercress mixture a little at a time, processing or stirring until the butter has been incorporated and the sauce is thick and smooth. Cover and chill.

8 Arrange the cucumber slices in overlapping rows along the length of the fish, so that they look like large fish scales. You can also slice the cucumber diagonally to produce longer slices for decoration. Trim the edges with scissors. Serve the fish, garnished with dill and lemon wedges, with the watercress sauce alongside.

Cook's Tip
Do not prepare the sauce more than a few hours ahead of serving as the watercress will discolour.

Per portion Energy 1044kcal/4323kJ; Protein 51.6g; Carbohydrate 1.4g, of which sugars 1.2g; Fat 92.4g, of which saturates 28.5g; Cholesterol 231mg; Calcium 135mg; Fibre 0.7g; Sodium 558mg.

Herrings in oatmeal

Herrings have a wonderfully strong flavour and are ideal for simple recipes. Traditional to the Northern Isles and the east coast, these herrings coated in oats make for hearty meals, and are also easy to prepare and cook.

Serves 4

175ml/6fl oz/¾ cup thick mayonnaise

15ml/1 tbsp Dijon mustard

7.5ml/1½ tsp tarragon vinegar

4 herrings, approximately 225g/8oz each

juice of 1 lemon

115g/4oz/generous 1 cup medium rolled oats

salt and ground black pepper

1 Place the mayonnaise in a small mixing bowl and add the mustard and vinegar. Mix thoroughly and then chill for a few minutes.

2 Place one fish at a time on a chopping board, cut side down, and open out. Press gently along the backbone with your thumbs. Turn the fish over and carefully lift away the backbone.

3 Squeeze lemon juice over both sides of the fish, then season with salt and ground black pepper. Fold the fish in half, skin side outwards.

4 Preheat the grill (broiler) to medium hot. Place the rolled oats on a plate then coat each herring evenly in the oats, pressing it in gently.

5 Place the herrings on a grill rack and grill (broil) the fish for 3–4 minutes on each side, until the skin is golden brown and crisp and the flesh flakes easily when the fish is cut into. Serve immediately on warmed plates with the mustard sauce handed round in a separate dish or bowl.

Per portion Energy 755kcal/3143kJ; Protein 36.7g; Carbohydrate 32.6g, of which sugars 0.6g; Fat 54g, of which saturates 9.3g; Cholesterol 98mg; Calcium 149mg; Fibre 3g; Sodium 459mg.

Mackerel with gooseberry relish

Off Scotland's west coast it is still possible to fish for mackerel yourself and quite often at the weekends part-time fishermen can be found selling fresh mackerel at the harbours. Mackerel is very good for you, and the tart gooseberries give you a serving of fruit too.

Serves 4

4 whole mackerel

60ml/4 tbsp olive oil

For the sauce

250g/9oz gooseberries

25g/1oz/2 tbsp soft light brown sugar

5ml/1 tsp wholegrain mustard

salt and ground black pepper

1 For the sauce, wash and trim the gooseberries and then roughly chop them, so there are some pieces larger than others.

2 Cook the gooseberries in a little water with the sugar in a small pan. A thick and chunky purée will form. Add the mustard and season to taste with salt and ground black pepper.

Cook's Tips
• Turn the grill (broiler) on well in advance as the fish need a fierce heat to cook quickly. If you like the fish but hate the smell, try barbecuing outside.
• The foil lining in the grill pan is to catch the smelly drips. Simply roll it up and throw it away afterwards, leaving a nice clean grill pan.

3 Preheat the grill (broiler) to high and line the grill pan with foil. Using a sharp knife, slash the fish two or three times down each side then season and brush with the olive oil.

4 Place the fish in the grill pan and grill (broil) for about 4 minutes on each side until cooked. You may need to cook them for a few minutes longer if they are particularly large. The slashes will open up to speed cooking and the skin should be lightly browned. To check that they are cooked properly, use a small sharp knife to pierce the skin and check for uncooked flesh.

5 Place the mackerel on warmed plates and spread generous dollops of the gooseberry relish over them. Pass the remaining sauce around at the table.

Per portion Energy 576kcal/2390kJ; Protein 38.1g; Carbohydrate 8.4g, of which sugars 8.4g; Fat 43.5g, of which saturates 8.2g; Cholesterol 108mg; Calcium 43mg; Fibre 1.5g; Sodium 128mg.

West coast fisherman's stew

Many of the little ports on the west coast of Scotland still land a small catch and often there will be a box of bits and pieces, perhaps a monkfish or some small haddock, a few prawns and small crabs. Therein lies a feast waiting to be made.

Serves 4

30ml/2 tbsp olive oil

1 large onion, roughly chopped

1 leek, roughly chopped

2 garlic cloves, crushed

450g/1lb ripe tomatoes, roughly chopped

5ml/1 tsp tomato purée (paste)

1.3kg/3lb fish bones

a piece of pared orange peel

a few parsley stalks and fennel fronds

1 bay leaf

250ml/8fl oz/1 cup dry white wine

whisky or pastis, such as Pernod (optional)

1kg/2¼lb mixed fish fillets, such as salmon, sole and haddock, cut into chunks, and prepared shellfish

salt and ground black pepper

chopped fresh parsley, to garnish

2 Put in the fish bones, orange peel, herbs and wine, and add a little salt and ground black pepper. Then add enough water just to cover. Bring to a gentle boil then reduce the heat and simmer for 30 minutes.

3 Strain the soup into a clean pan, pressing the juices out of the solid ingredients with the back of a spoon.

4 Bring the liquid back to the boil and check for seasoning and texture. If you like, add a splash of whisky or Pernod. The fish takes just minutes to cook so add the firmer, larger pieces first, such as monkfish or salmon and mussels in the shell, and end with delicate scallops or prawn (shrimp) tails. Do not allow the stew to boil once you add the fish.

5 Serve in warmed soup plates, garnished with chopped fresh parsley.

1 Heat the olive oil in a large pan then add the onion and leek, and sweat until soft. Add the garlic, tomatoes and tomato purée, and cook for 5 minutes.

Per portion Energy 341kcal/1432kJ; Protein 47.5g; Carbohydrate 6.5g, of which sugars 5.8g; Fat 7.8g, of which saturates 1.2g; Cholesterol 115mg; Calcium 53mg; Fibre 2.3g; Sodium 165mg.

Pale smoked haddock flan

The classic combination of potatoes and smoked fish is reworked in pastry. Always ask your fishmonger for 'pale' smoked rather than 'yellow' haddock as the latter tends to have been dyed to look bright and often has not been smoked properly at all.

Serves 4

For the pastry

225g/8oz/2 cups plain (all-purpose) flour

pinch of salt

115g/4oz/1½ cup cold butter, cut into chunks

cold water, to mix

For the filling

2 pale smoked haddock fillets (approximately 200g/7oz)

600ml/1 pint/2½ cups full-fat (whole) milk

3–4 black peppercorns

sprig of fresh thyme

150ml/¼ pint/⅔ cup double (heavy) cream

2 eggs

200g/7oz potatoes, peeled and diced

ground black pepper

1 Preheat the oven to 200°C/400°F/Gas 6. Use a food processor to make the pastry. Put the flour, salt and butter into the food processor bowl and process until the mixture resembles fine breadcrumbs.

2 Pour in a little cold water (you will need about 40ml/8 tsp but see Cook's Tip) and continue to process until the mixture forms a ball. If this takes longer than 30 seconds add a little more water.

3 Take the pastry ball out of the food processor, wrap in clear film (plastic wrap) and leave to rest in a cool place for about 30 minutes.

4 Roll out the dough and use to line a 20cm/8in flan tin (quiche pan). Prick the base of the pastry all over with a fork then bake blind in the preheated oven for 20 minutes.

5 Put the haddock in a pan with the milk, peppercorns and thyme. Poach for 10 minutes. Remove the fish from the pan and flake into small chunks. Allow the poaching liquor to cool.

6 Whisk the cream and eggs together thoroughly, then whisk in the cooled poaching liquid.

Variation
This recipe is also delicious if you add hard-boiled eggs, chopped into quarters or eighths before adding the potatoes.

7 Layer the flan case with the flaked fish and diced potato, seasoning with black pepper.

8 Pour the cream mixture over the top. Put the flan in the oven and bake for 40 minutes, until lightly browned on top and set.

Cook's Tip
Different flours absorb water at different rates. A traditional rule of thumb is to use the same number of teaspoons of water as the number of ounces of flour, but some flours will require less water and others more, so add the water gradually. If you add too much water, the pastry will become unworkable and you will need to add more flour.

Per portion Energy 734kcal/3064kJ; Protein 23.8g; Carbohydrate 58.4g, of which sugars 8.2g; Fat 46.8g, of which saturates 27.9g; Cholesterol 225mg; Calcium 280mg; Fibre 2.3g; Sodium 636mg.

Meat, poultry and game

Scottish beef is renowned throughout the world for its superb quality and fine taste. Excellent steaks and prime cuts of beef constitute a large part of the cuisine, either in classic pies and stews or with sumptuous sauces made with seasonal ingredients. Lamb and pork dishes are also enjoyed, especially in the Lowlands. Traditionally, poultry was reared in the backyard of most homes, and game was available to rich and poor alike. These days venison is farmed, so it is widely available for making a variety of wonderful Scottish dishes.

Haggis with clapshot cake

Haggis is probably the best known of all classic Scottish dishes, not least because of the famous Burns poem which is recited the world over in front of a haggis at suppers celebrating the poet. This is the traditional haggis recipe served with turnip and potato clapshot – a variation on the 'haggis with neeps and tatties' theme.

Serves 4

1 large haggis, approximately 800g/1¾lb

450g/1lb peeled turnip or swede (rutabaga)

225g/8oz peeled potatoes

120ml/4fl oz/½ cup milk

1 garlic clove, crushed with 5ml/1 tsp salt

175ml/6fl oz/¾ cup double (heavy) cream

freshly grated nutmeg

ground black pepper

butter, for greasing

1 Preheat the oven to 180°C/350°F/ Gas 4. Wrap the haggis in foil, covering it completely and folding over the edges of the foil.

Cook's Tip
If you are serving haggis on Burns Night (January 25th), you need to bring the haggis whole to the table on a platter and cut it open reciting the famous Burns poem. This traditional ceremony takes place each year in honour of Robert Burns, the celebrated Scottish poet.

2 Place the haggis in a roasting pan with about 2.5cm/1in water. Heat through in the preheated oven for 30–40 minutes.

3 Slice the turnip or swede and potatoes quite finely. A mandolin or food processor is quite handy for the turnip or swede as both vegetables tend to be hard and difficult to cut finely with a knife.

4 Put the sliced vegetables in a large pan and add the milk and garlic. Stir gently and continuously over a low heat until the potatoes begin to break down and exude their starch and the liquid thickens slightly.

5 Add the cream and nutmeg and grind some black pepper into the mixture. Stir gently but thoroughly. Slowly bring to the boil, reduce the heat and simmer gently for a few minutes.

6 Butter a deep round 18cm/7in dish or a small roasting pan. Transfer the vegetable mixture to the dish or pan. It shouldn't come up too high as it will rise slightly and bubble.

7 Bake in the oven for about 1 hour, or until you can push a knife easily through the cake. The top should be nicely browned by this time. If it is becoming too brown on top, cover it with foil and continue baking. If it is not browned enough after 1 hour of cooking, place it under a hot grill (broiler) for a few minutes.

8 Remove the foil from the haggis, place on a warmed serving dish and bring out to the table for your guests to witness the cutting. Use a sharp knife to cut through the skin then spoon out the haggis on to warmed plates. Serve the clapshot cake in slices with the haggis, spooning any juices over.

Per portion Energy 918kcal/3819kJ; Protein 24.9g; Carbohydrate 55.3g, of which sugars 8.5g; Fat 67.9g, of which saturates 30.2g; Cholesterol 244mg; Calcium 180mg; Fibre 3.1g; Sodium 1586mg.

Angus pasties

Aberdeen Angus beef is the traditional filling for pasties, as it is such a well-known breed, but any really good-quality beef may be used. These pasties are perfect served either cold or warmed for lunch or as a snack, and make great picnic food.

Makes 10

For the pastry

900g/2lb/8 cups plain (all-purpose) flour

225g/8oz/1 cup butter

225g/8oz/1cup lard or white cooking fat

pinch of salt

For the filling

1.2kg/2½lb rump (round) steak

225g/8oz/1¾ cups beef suet (US chilled, grated shortening)

5 onions, finely chopped

salt and ground black pepper

1 Preheat the oven to 200°C/400°F/ Gas 6. Using a mixer, place the flour in the mixing bowl and blend in the butter and lard or white cooking fat using the dough hook. Add salt and mix to a stiff dough, adding water gradually as needed. Leave the pastry ball to rest in clear film (plastic wrap) for 30 minutes.

2 Meanwhile, trim the meat of any excess fat and cut into 1cm/½in squares. Chop the suet finely then mix with the meat and onions. Season.

3 Divide the pastry into ten equal sized pieces. Roll out each piece into an oval, not too thinly, and divide the meat mixture among them at one end, leaving an edge for sealing. Dampen the edges of each oval with cold water and fold the pastry over the filling.

4 Seal carefully – use a fork to make sure the edges are stuck together securely. Make a hole in the top of each pasty. Place on a greased baking sheet and bake in the preheated oven for 45 minutes. Serve hot, or allow to cool and refrigerate.

Per portion Energy 1131kcal/4714kJ; Protein 37.7g; Carbohydrate 84.8g, of which sugars 4.5g; Fat 74.5g, of which saturates 37.9g; Cholesterol 171mg; Calcium 162mg; Fibre 3.9g; Sodium 232mg.

Dundee beef stew

Dundee is famously known as the home of marmalade, and this stew is flavoured with it. Red wine possibly also came into Dundee's busy port, though the majority must have come into Leith, the larger port for Edinburgh further south. Serve with mashed potatoes.

Serves 4

900g/2lb stewing beef

50g/2oz/½ cup plain (all-purpose) flour

2.5ml/½ tsp paprika

30ml/2 tbsp vegetable oil

225g/8oz onions, peeled and chopped

50g/2oz/½ stick butter

100g/4oz button (white) mushrooms, quartered

2 garlic cloves, crushed with a little salt

15ml/1 tbsp bitter marmalade

300ml/½ pint/1¼ cups red wine

150ml/¼ pint/⅔ cup beef stock

salt and ground black pepper

1 Preheat the oven to 180°C/350°F/ Gas 4. Cut the meat into 2.5cm/1in cubes. Season the plain flour with salt, black pepper and the paprika. Spread the seasoned flour on a tray and coat the meat in it.

3 Transfer the meat to a casserole. Brown the onions in the original pan, adding a little butter if they seem too dry. Add to the casserole.

2 Heat a large pan, add the vegetable oil and brown the meat. Do this in batches if your pan is small.

4 Keeping the pan hot, add the rest of the butter and brown the mushrooms then transfer to the casserole.

5 Add the rest of the ingredients to the casserole and bring to the boil, stirring to combine the marmalade and evenly distribute the meat and mushrooms. Cover the casserole and place in the preheated oven for about 3 hours, until the meat is tender. Serve with creamy mashed potatoes.

Per portion Energy 544kcal/2276kJ; Protein 53.3g; Carbohydrate 17.1g, of which sugars 6.2g; Fat 24.1g, of which saturates 10.4g; Cholesterol 177mg; Calcium 53mg; Fibre 1.5g; Sodium 242mg.

Griddled loin of lamb with barley risotto

A loin of lamb is taken from the back or the saddle, and it should be completely clear of fat or gristle so you are getting pure meat. Good lamb needs little cooking – remember to take it out of the refrigerator well before you cook it to raise it to room temperature as it will then cook more quickly. Always pat the meat dry before putting it on a griddle pan.

Serves 4

a little olive oil

750ml/1¼ pints/3 cups chicken stock

75g/3oz/6 tbsp butter

1 onion, finely chopped

225g/8oz/1 cup barley

50g/2oz Bonnet cheese

3 loins of lamb

salt and ground black pepper

virgin olive oil, to serve

1 Prepare a cast-iron ridged griddle or heavy pan by brushing it with olive oil. Bring the stock to the boil. Melt the butter in a pan, and sweat the onion.

2 Add the barley to the pan and stir to coat well with the olive oil.

3 Add about one-third of the stock. Bring to the boil then reduce the heat, stirring all the time until the liquid is absorbed by the barley. Add half of the remaining stock and continue to stir and absorb. Finally add the rest of the stock, stirring all the time. You will create a thick, creamy mixture, with the barley still having a little 'bite' to it. You may need more or less liquid depending on the barley; if you need more just add boiling water.

4 Grate the cheese and add to the barley when it has absorbed all the stock. Stir in well, season with salt and ground black pepper, and keep warm.

5 Heat the griddle or heavy pan until very hot. Brush the lamb with olive oil and season with salt and pepper. Sear the lamb quickly all over to brown it, then reduce the heat and cook for a further 8 minutes, turning occasionally. Leave it in a warm place to rest for 5 minutes.

6 Serve by carving thickish slices from each loin at an angle. You should get four slices from each loin, giving three per person. Add a splash of virgin olive oil to the risotto, place a mound of risotto on each warmed plate and prop the slices of lamb on it.

Per portion Energy 827kcal/3460kJ; Protein 49.8g; Carbohydrate 53.2g, of which sugars 2.2g; Fat 47.7g, of which saturates 25.2g; Cholesterol 223mg; Calcium 55mg; Fibre 0.5g; Sodium 348mg.

Braised shoulder of lamb with dulse

Dulse is a sea vegetable or seaweed used traditionally for flavouring dishes, especially lamb and mutton. On the Outer Hebrides the sheep will graze near the seashore and will actually eat the seaweed as well. Soay sheep, a hardy breed, feed almost exclusively on it and the flavour of their meat is improved by it too.

Serves 4

1.8kg/4lb shoulder of lamb, bone in and well trimmed of fat

30ml/2 tbsp vegetable oil

250g/9oz onions

25g/1oz/2 tbsp butter

pinch of caster (superfine) sugar

500ml/scant pint water

50g/2oz dried dulse

1 bay leaf

salt and ground black pepper

1 Preheat the oven to 180°C/350°F/ Gas 4, if necessary (see Step 5). Season the lamb all over.

2 Place a pan, big enough to hold the lamb and with a lid, on the stove. When hot, add the oil and brown the lamb all over. This can be a little difficult, as there are bits you really can't reach with the bone in, but brown as much as you can.

Cook's Tip
Press the onion hard through the sieve when straining the sauce, and if it is a bit thin boil it for a short while to reduce slightly.

3 Remove the lamb from the pan and drain off the excess fat, reserving it in case you need extra for the sauce. Peel the onions, cut in half and slice – not too finely – into half rounds.

4 Return the pan to a medium heat and add the butter. When it has melted completely, add the sliced onions with the sugar and a little salt and ground black pepper. Stir to coat with the butter then colour, without burning, for about 9 minutes.

5 Place the lamb on top of the onions, add the water, dulse and bay leaf, and season again. Cover and bring to the boil. Cook for 2 hours either over a very low heat or in the oven if the pan will fit and has ovenproof handles.

6 Remove the lamb from the pan, set aside and keep warm. Check the sauce for consistency, adding some of the reserved fat if necessary. Strain and adjust the seasoning. Slice the lamb and serve with the sauce.

Per portion Energy 677kcal/2808kJ; Protein 43.5g; Carbohydrate 5.2g, of which sugars 3.7g; Fat 53.7g, of which saturates 23.7g; Cholesterol 194mg; Calcium 48mg; Fibre 1.3g; Sodium 188mg.

Roast venison

Venison has been eaten in Scotland for generations, by kings, lairds and ordinary people, hunted and poached in equal measure. Today the wild deer are culled regularly to keep the stocks healthy and excellent wild meat is available through game dealers. There are also a number of deer farms, which produce meat of a very high quality.

Serves 4

1 venison haunch, approximately 2.75kg/6lb

30ml/2 tbsp olive oil

25g/1oz/2 tbsp butter

225g/8oz bacon, diced

salt and ground black pepper

For the marinade

1 onion, sliced

2 carrots, peeled and sliced

60ml/4 tbsp olive oil

1 bottle red wine

2 garlic cloves, crushed

1 bay leaf

5 black peppercorns

sprig of rosemary

6 juniper berries

For the sauce

15ml/1 tbsp plain (all-purpose) flour

15ml/1 tbsp butter, softened

150ml/¼ pint/⅔ cup port

15ml/1 tbsp rowan jelly

1 Marinate the meat two days before cooking. Cook the onion and carrots in the olive oil, without allowing them to colour. Then put the mixture into a non-metallic container that is large enough to hold the venison. Add the other ingredients. Put the haunch in and leave for two days, turning regularly to coat all sides.

2 When ready to cook, preheat the oven to 160°C/325°F/Gas 3. Remove the haunch from the marinade and dry with kitchen paper.

3 Put a large casserole, into which the haunch will fit with the lid on, over a high heat and add the oil and butter. Brown the bacon and then the haunch, browning it all over.

4 In another pan, reduce the marinade by half by boiling it rapidly and then strain over the haunch. Cover and cook for 30 minutes per 450g/1lb. When cooked, remove and keep warm, covered in foil so it does not dry out.

5 Strain the juices into a pan and boil rapidly. Make a beurre manié by mixing the flour and butter together and whisk it into the boiling liquor. Simmer until reduced by half. Add the port and the rowan jelly, adjust the seasoning, if necessary, and serve.

Per portion Energy 978kcal/4132kJ; Protein 167.1g; Carbohydrate 11.1g, of which sugars 7.3g; Fat 25.2g, of which saturates 8.8g; Cholesterol 383mg; Calcium 52mg; Fibre 0.2g; Sodium 442mg.

Smoked venison with garlic mashed potatoes

Smoked venison is one of Scotland's lesser known treasures, and it can be used in many different ways. The best smoked venison is, of course, from wild animals taken from the moors and hills. The only smoker in Scotland to smoke wild venison is Rannoch Smokery in Perthshire. This warming dish makes an ideal supper or lunch.

Serves 4

675g/1½lb peeled potatoes

175ml/6fl oz/¾ cup milk

1 garlic clove

10ml/2 tsp sea salt

olive oil, for greasing and to serve

75ml/2½fl oz/⅓ cup double (heavy) cream

115g/4oz sliced smoked venison

salad leaves, to garnish

1 Preheat the oven to 180°C/350°F/ Gas 4. Slice the potatoes thinly using a sharp knife or mandolin. Place in a pan and pour in the milk.

2 Crush the garlic with the sea salt using the side of a knife. Stir the mixture into the potatoes. Bring to the boil over a gentle heat, stirring occasionally, until the starch comes out of the potatoes and the milk begins to thicken.

3 Grease the inside of a large gratin dish with a little olive oil.

4 Add the cream to the potatoes and, stirring gently so the potatoes don't break up, combine well. Allow to just come to the boil again then pour the mixture carefully into the ovenproof gratin dish.

5 Place the dish in the preheated oven for about 1 hour until lightly browned and tender.

6 To serve, scoop the potato on to warmed plates and put a pile of smoked venison on top, adding a splash of olive oil over each serving. Garnish with salad leaves.

Cook's Tips
• Use good tasty potatoes, such as King Edward or Maris Piper, for this dish (US russet or Idaho).
• If you are feeling generous, you could use more smoked venison.

Per portion Energy 281kcal/1180kJ; Protein 15.6g; Carbohydrate 29.5g, of which sugars 4.5g; Fat 12g, of which saturates 6.1g; Cholesterol 25mg; Calcium 80mg; Fibre 1.7g; Sodium 1050mg.

Chicken and mushroom pie

Chicken pie is a favourite throughout Scotland, especially in the Lowlands where farmyard chickens provide a plentiful supply of fresh, free-range birds. If you can find them, use wild mushrooms, such as ceps or field blewits, to intensify the flavours.

Serves 6

50g/2oz/¼ cup butter

30ml/2 tbsp plain (all-purpose) flour

250ml/8fl oz/1 cup hot chicken stock

60ml/4 tbsp single (light) cream

1 onion, coarsely chopped

2 carrots, sliced

2 celery sticks, coarsely chopped

50g/2oz fresh (preferably wild) mushrooms, quartered

450g/1lb cooked chicken meat, cubed

50g/2oz/½ cup fresh or frozen peas

salt and ground black pepper

beaten egg, to glaze

For the pastry

225g/8oz/2 cups plain (all-purpose) flour

1.5ml/¼ tsp salt

115g/4oz/½ cup cold butter, diced

65g/2½oz/⅓ cup white vegetable fat (shortening), diced

90–120ml/6–8 tbsp chilled water

1 To make the pastry, sift the flour and salt into a bowl. Rub in the butter and white vegetable fat until the mixture resembles breadcrumbs. Sprinkle with 90ml/6 tbsp chilled water and mix until the dough holds together. If the dough is too crumbly, add a little more water, 15ml/1 tbsp at a time.

2 Gather the dough into a ball and flatten it into a round. Wrap in clear film (plastic wrap) so that it is airtight and chill in the refrigerator for at least 30 minutes.

3 Preheat the oven to 190°C/375°F/ Gas 5. To make the filling, melt half the butter in a heavy pan over a low heat. Whisk in the flour and cook until bubbling, whisking constantly. Add the hot stock and whisk over a medium heat until the mixture boils. Cook for 2–3 minutes, then whisk in the cream. Season to taste with salt and ground black pepper, and set aside.

4 Heat the remaining butter in a large non-stick frying pan and cook the onion and carrots over a low heat for about 5 minutes. Add the celery and mushrooms and cook for a further 5 minutes, until they have softened. Add the cooked chicken and peas and stir in thoroughly.

5 Add the chicken mixture to the hot cream sauce and stir to mix. Adjust the seasoning if necessary. Spoon the mixture into a 2.5 litre/4 pint/2½ quart oval baking dish.

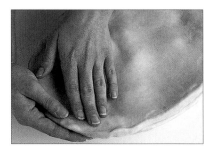

6 Roll out the pastry on a floured surface to a thickness of about 3mm/⅛in. Cut out an oval 2.5cm/1in larger all around than the dish. Lay the pastry over the filling. Gently press around the edge of the dish to seal, then trim off the excess pastry. Crimp the edge of the pastry by pushing the forefinger of one hand into the edge and, using the thumb and forefinger of the other hand, pinch the pastry. Continue all round the pastry edge.

7 Press together the pastry trimmings and roll out again. Cut out mushroom shapes with a sharp knife and stick them on to the pastry lid with a little of the beaten egg. Glaze the lid with beaten egg and cut several slits in the pastry to allow the steam to escape.

8 Bake the pie in the preheated oven for about 30 minutes, until the pastry has browned. Serve hot.

Cook's Tip
Using a combination of butter and white vegetable fat gives shortcrust pastry a lovely crumbly texture.

Per portion Energy 600kcal/2501kJ; Protein 23.7g; Carbohydrate 38.8g, of which sugars 3.7g; Fat 40g, of which saturates 21.8g; Cholesterol 132mg; Calcium 92mg; Fibre 2.7g; Sodium 226mg.

Chicken with summer vegetables and tarragon

This is an all-in-the-pot dish, with the chicken cooking liquor providing the stock for the rest of the cooking and the sauce. Summer vegetables are wonderfully packed with flavour, and it is up to you to pick the selection you prefer.

Serves 4

1.8kg/4lb boiling fowl (stewing chicken)

1 onion, peeled, studded with 6 cloves

1 bay leaf

a sprig each of thyme and parsley

10 black peppercorns

12 small potatoes, washed

8 small shallots, peeled

vegetables of your choice, such as carrots, courgettes (zucchini), broad (fava) beans and peas

25g/1oz/2 tbsp butter

30ml/2 tbsp plain (all-purpose) flour

60ml/4 tbsp chopped fresh tarragon

1 Wash the chicken and dry with kitchen paper. Place in a large pan with the onion, bay leaf, thyme, parsley and peppercorns, with water to cover. Stir to mix in all the ingredients and bring to the boil over a high heat. Reduce the heat and simmer gently for 1½ hours. Skim off the froth occasionally as the bird is boiling and make sure the chicken is covered, topping up with water if necessary.

2 Meanwhile prepare all the vegetables and place them in rows on a tray in order of cooking time, from the longest to the shortest.

3 Once cooked remove the chicken from the pan and keep warm. Remove all the seasonings, either with a slotted spoon or by straining the mixture, then bring the cooking liquor back to the boil, skimming off any fat that may have appeared on the top.

4 Start to cook the vegetables in the liqour, putting the potatoes in first for a few minutes, then adding the shallots and carrots, if using, and finally the green vegetables that take no time at all – mangetouts, for example, should go in when the potatoes are cooked. When the vegetables are cooked, place the chicken on a serving dish and surround with all the vegetables.

5 In a small pan melt the butter, add the flour and stir to create a roux. Slowly add some liquor from the large pan until a sauce is created – about 600ml/1 pint/2½ cups – and allow to simmer for a few minutes to reduce down and strengthen the flavour. At the last moment stir in the chopped fresh tarragon then ladle the sauce over the chicken and vegetables. Bring to the table and serve immediately.

Per portion Energy 713kcal/2973kJ; Protein 51.2g; Carbohydrate 39.3g, of which sugars 13g; Fat 40g, of which saturates 12.9g; Cholesterol 261mg; Calcium 103mg; Fibre 5.4g; Sodium 251mg.

Grey partridge with lentils and sausage

Grey partridge is indigenous to Scotland, although it is often called the English partridge, and is slightly smaller than the European red-legged variety. The wonderful rich flavour is complemented by the lovely earthy flavour of the Puy lentils.

Serves 4

450g/1lb/2 cups Puy lentils

75g/3oz/6 tbsp butter

15ml/1 tbsp vegetable oil

4 grey partridges

2 venison sausages

1 garlic clove, peeled but left whole

250ml/8fl oz/1 cup stock

salt and ground black pepper

1 Preheat the oven to 180°C/350°F/ Gas 4. Wash the lentils then simmer them in water for about 10 minutes to soften slightly. Drain then set aside.

2 Melt one-third of the butter with the oil in a large ovenproof frying pan and place the partridges, breast side down, in the pan. Brown both breasts lightly.

3 Set the partridges on their backs, season lightly with salt and ground black pepper and cook in the preheated oven for 15 minutes.

4 When cooked, remove the partridges from the oven, allow to cool for a few minutes then remove the legs. Keep the rest warm.

5 Put the large frying pan back on the hob and brown the two sausages. Add the Puy lentils and garlic and stir to coat in the juices from the partridges and the sausages. Then add the stock and simmer for a few minutes. Place the partridge legs on top of the lentil mixture and return to the oven for a further 15 minutes.

6 Remove the pan from the oven and set aside the partridge legs and sausages. Discard the garlic. Season the lentils with salt and ground black pepper, and if there is still a lot of liquid remaining, boil over a low heat to evaporate a little of the excess moisture. Then, off the heat, gradually swirl in the remaining butter.

7 Remove the breasts from the carcasses and set aside. Cut the sausages into pieces and stir into the lentil mixture.

8 To serve, place a leg on individual warmed plates, put the lentils on top and then the breast, sliced lengthways, on top of the lentils.

Per portion Energy 1309kcal/5495kJ; Protein 152.1g; Carbohydrate 59.4g, of which sugars 2.2g; Fat 53g, of which saturates 20.1g; Cholesterol 55mg; Calcium 255mg; Fibre 10.2g; Sodium 761mg.

Roast young grouse

As with venison, rowan jelly goes well with this meat. Young grouse can be identified by their pliable breastbone, legs and feet, and their claws will be sharp. They have very little fat so bacon is used here to protect the breasts during the initial roasting.

Serves 2

2 young grouse

6 rashers (strips) bacon

2 sprigs of rowanberries or 1 lemon, quartered, plus 30ml/2 tbsp extra rowanberries (optional)

50g/2oz/¼ cup butter

150ml/¼ pint/⅔ cup red wine

150ml/¼ pint/⅔ cup water

5ml/1 tsp rowan jelly

salt and ground black pepper

Cook's Tip
Grouse is usually served with bread sauce and game chips, but Skirlie is good too.

1 Preheat the oven to 200°C/400°F/ Gas 6. Wipe the grouse with kitchen paper and place in a roasting pan. Lay the bacon over the breasts.

2 If you have rowanberries, place one sprig in the cavity of each grouse as well as a little butter. Otherwise put a lemon quarter in each cavity as well as a little butter.

3 Roast the grouse in the preheated oven for 10 minutes.

4 Remove the bacon and pour in the wine. Return the grouse to the oven for 10 minutes.

5 Baste the birds with the pan juices and cook them for a further 5 minutes. Remove the birds from the pan and keep warm.

6 Add the water and rowan jelly to the pan and simmer gently until the jelly melts. Strain into another pan, add the rowanberries, if using, and simmer until the sauce just begins to thicken. Season with salt and ground black pepper, then serve the sauce with the grouse.

Per portion Energy 423kcal/1763kJ; Protein 43.8g; Carbohydrate 1.5g, of which sugars 1.5g; Fat 24g, of which saturates 10.8g; Cholesterol 51mg; Calcium 43mg; Fibre 0g; Sodium 902mg.

Pan-fried pheasant with oatmeal and cream sauce

Rolled oats are often used for coating fish before pan-frying, but this treatment is equally good with tender poultry, game and other meats. Sweet, slightly tangy redcurrant jelly is used to bind the oatmeal to the tender pheasant breast fillets.

Serves 4

115g/4oz/generous 1 cup medium rolled oats

4 skinless, boneless pheasant breasts

45ml/3 tbsp redcurrant jelly, melted

50g/2oz/¼ cup butter

15ml/1 tbsp olive oil

45ml/3 tbsp wholegrain mustard

300ml/½ pint/1¼ cups double (heavy) cream

salt and ground black pepper

1 Place the rolled oats on a plate and season with salt and ground black pepper. Brush the skinned pheasant breasts with the melted redcurrant jelly, then turn them in the oats to coat evenly. Shake off any excess oats and set aside.

2 Heat the butter and oil in a frying pan until foaming. Add the pheasant breasts and cook over a high heat, turning frequently, until they are golden brown on all sides. Reduce the heat to medium and cook for a further 8–10 minutes, turning once or twice, until the meat is thoroughly cooked.

3 Add the mustard and cream, stirring to combine with the cooking juices. Bring slowly to the boil then simmer for 10 minutes over a low heat, or until the sauce has thickened to a good consistency. Serve immediately.

Per portion Energy 847kcal/3520kJ; Protein 37.1g; Carbohydrate 30.1g, of which sugars 9.1g; Fat 59g, of which saturates 35.1g; Cholesterol 129mg; Calcium 105mg; Fibre 2g; Sodium 205mg.

Saddle of rabbit with asparagus

Some of the best asparagus comes from near Glamis in Angus in the east of the country where a little extra sunlight produces stems with juicy, succulent flavours. This is not like the white asparagus of Europe, which is grown underground, but a better-flavoured, more satisfying green variety, which grows above the soil.

Serves 4

2 saddles of rabbit

75g/3oz/6 tbsp butter

sprig of fresh rosemary

45ml/3 tbsp olive oil

10 asparagus spears

200ml/7fl oz/scant 1 cup chicken stock, plus extra for cooking the asparagus (see Step 5)

salt and ground black pepper

1 Preheat the oven to 200°C/400°F/ Gas 6. Trim the rabbit saddles with a sharp knife, removing the membrane and the belly flaps.

2 Heat an ovenproof pan then add 50g/2oz/4 tbsp of the butter. Season the saddles and brown them lightly all over, by frying them gently in the butter for a few minutes on each side.

3 Tuck the rosemary underneath the saddles, with the fillets facing up, and put in the oven for 10 minutes.

4 Meanwhile, in a second pan, heat the olive oil then add the asparagus spears. Coat them in the oil then leave them to sweat gently for a few minutes.

5 Add enough stock to just cover the asparagus and bring to a gentle boil. Allow the liquid to evaporate to a light glaze and the asparagus will be cooked.

6 Remove the rabbit from the oven and leave to rest for 5 minutes. Remove any fat from the pan then add the measured stock. Bring to the boil, scraping up any bits from the base of the pan. Reduce the liquid by about a half, then remove from the heat and whisk in the remaining butter. Strain through a sieve and set aside.

7 Take the meat off the saddles in slices lengthways and place on a warmed serving dish. Serve with the asparagus on top and the sauce spooned over.

Per portion Energy 406kcal/1684kJ; Protein 33.7g; Carbohydrate 0.6g, of which sugars 0.6g; Fat 29.8g, of which saturates 13.4g; Cholesterol 146mg; Calcium 43mg; Fibre 0.4g; Sodium 215mg.

Roast hare with beetroot and crowdie

Hares are not the easiest of things to get hold of but in some parts of Scotland they are often available. This sauce goes well with venison too. Crowdie is a cream cheese made on every homestead up to the middle of the last century. For a less rich dish you could use plain yogurt in place of the crowdie at the end.

Serves 4

2 saddles of hare

10ml/2 tsp olive oil

350g/12oz cooked beetroot (beets)

30ml/2 tbsp chopped shallot

30ml/2 tbsp white wine vinegar

50g/2oz/¼ cup crowdie

5ml/1 tsp English mustard

salt and ground black pepper

For the marinade

600ml/1 pint/2½ cups red wine

1 carrot, finely diced

1 onion, finely diced

generous pinch of mixed herbs

pinch of salt

8 peppercorns

8 juniper berries

2 cloves

1 Using a flexible knife, remove the membrane covering the saddles. Mix all the ingredients for the marinade together and coat the saddles then leave for one day, turning occasionally.

2 Preheat the oven to 240°C/475°F/ Gas 9. Take out and dry the saddles with kitchen paper. Strain the marinade through a sieve and set aside.

3 Heat the olive oil in a large ovenproof pan. Brown the saddles all over then cook in the preheated oven for 10–15 minutes. They should still be pink. Leave in a warm place to rest.

4 Remove most of the fat from the pan then add the beetroot. Cook for 1–2 minutes then add the shallot and cook for about 2 minutes to soften.

5 Add the vinegar and 30ml/2 tbsp of the marinade and stir in thoroughly. Reduce the liquid until a coating texture is nearly achieved. Reduce the heat to low and add the crowdie. Whisk it in until completely melted, then add the mustard and season to taste. Set aside and keep warm.

6 To serve, remove the fillets from the top and bottom of the saddles and slice lengthways. Place on four warmed plates and arrange the beetroot mixture on top. Reheat the sauce, without boiling, and hand round separately.

Per portion Energy 352kcal/1471kJ; Protein 41g; Carbohydrate 9.6g, of which sugars 8.7g; Fat 13.1g, of which saturates 6.5g; Cholesterol 136mg; Calcium 84mg; Fibre 1.9g; Sodium 255mg.

Loin of wild boar with bog myrtle

Wild boar used to roam the hills of Scotland centuries ago and when the kings of Scotland came for their summer holidays to Falkland Palace, Fife, they would go out hunting for them. Today they no longer exist in the wild but are farmed as a rare breed of pig. Their meat is similar to pork in that it has a sweetness to it, and the crackling is fantastic.

Serves 4

1 loin of wild boar, approximately 2.75kg/6lb

10ml/2 tsp salt

1 onion, roughly chopped

1 carrot, peeled and roughly chopped

150ml/¼ pint/⅔ cup dry vermouth

10ml/2 tsp English mustard

handful of bog myrtle, or a few sprigs of fresh rosemary, if you prefer

salt and ground black pepper

1 Ask your butcher to take the loin off the bone and then to tie it back on and to make 2cm/¾in cuts through the skin from top to bottom at 5cm/2in intervals. This will make the crackling easier to slice when you come to carve. Allow the loin to sit at room temperature for at least an hour prior to cooking. Preheat the oven to 220°C/425°F/Gas 7.

2 Rub the salt all over the skin of the boar, easing it slightly into the cuts made by the butcher.

3 Place the chopped vegetables and herbs in a lightly oiled roasting pan.

4 Put the loin on top of the vegetables and herbs, with the skin facing up, and roast in the oven for 40 minutes.

5 Reduce the oven temperature to 180°C/350°F/Gas 4 and cook for another 40 minutes. Remove from the oven and cut the meat from the bones – this should just be a matter of cutting the string. Set the meat aside to rest for at least 20 minutes.

6 Meanwhile make the gravy. Pour or spoon off the excess fat from the roasting pan but try to retain the juices, which will be under the fat.

7 Put the roasting pan on the stove over a low heat and add the vermouth and mustard. Stir well to mix thoroughly, scraping the base of the pan to incorporate the cooked flavours.

8 Just as it comes to the boil, pour the gravy into a clean pan, along with the bones, herbs and vegetables. Swill out the roasting pan with a little water and add this to the new pan, making sure that you have all the juices. Simmer the gravy in the new pan for about 5 minutes.

9 Remove the bones and strain the juices into the gravy pan. Test the seasoning, adding salt and ground black pepper if necessary.

10 Serve the loin in slices, each slice with a strip of the crackling, and pass around the gravy in a separate dish.

Cook's Tip
The crackling is particularly good and can be broken off in chunks because of the cuts made prior to cooking. The meat can be carved separately.

Per portion Energy 530kcal/2221kJ; Protein 81.9g; Carbohydrate 6.7g, of which sugars 5.7g; Fat 15.5g, of which saturates 5.3g; Cholesterol 236mg; Calcium 109mg; Fibre 1.9g; Sodium 1309mg.

Side dishes

Almost as tasty as the main course itself, the vegetables and salads in Scottish cuisine provide an often healthy or hearty accompaniment to every meal. The richly flavoured green vegetables, including kale, chard, spinach and cabbage, are excellent served on their own or with a sauce. No meal is complete, however, without those robust root vegetables: turnip, swede, parsnip, carrot and the versatile favourite, the potato.

Clapshot

This root vegetable dish is excellent with haggis or on top of shepherd's pie in place of just potato. Turnips give an earthy flavour, and swede introduces a sweet accent. It is also slightly less heavy than mashed potato, which is good for a lighter meal or supper.

Serves 4

450g/1lb potatoes

450g/1lb turnips or swede (rutabaga)

50g/2oz/¼ cup butter

50ml/2fl oz/¼ cup milk

5ml/1 tsp freshly grated nutmeg

30ml/2 tbsp chopped fresh parsley

salt and ground black pepper

1 Peel the potatoes and turnips or swede, then cut them into evenly sized small chunks. You will need a large sharp knife for the turnips.

2 Place the chopped vegetables in a pan and cover with cold water. Bring to the boil over a medium heat, then reduce the heat and simmer until both vegetables are cooked, which will take about 15–20 minutes. Test the vegetables by pushing the point of a sharp knife into one of the cubes; if it goes in easily and the cube begins to break apart, then it is cooked.

3 Drain the vegetables through a colander. Return to the pan and allow them to dry out for a few minutes over a low heat, stirring occasionally to prevent any from sticking to the base of the pan.

4 Melt the butter with the milk in a small pan over a low heat. Mash the dry potato and turnip or swede mixture, then add the milk mixture. Grate in the nutmeg, add the parsley, mix thoroughly and season to taste. Serve immediately with roast meat or game.

Per portion Energy 204kcal/852kJ; Protein 3.4g; Carbohydrate 24.1g, of which sugars 7.2g; Fat 11.2g, of which saturates 6.8g; Cholesterol 27mg; Calcium 78mg; Fibre 3.8g; Sodium 111mg.

Skirlie

Oatmeal has been a staple in Scotland for centuries. Skirlie is a simple preparation and can be used for stuffings or as an accompaniment, and is especially good with roast meats. It is traditionally cooked in lard but many people prefer butter.

Serves 4

50g/2oz/¼ cup butter

1 onion, finely chopped

175g/6oz/scant 2 cups medium rolled oats

salt and ground black pepper

Variation
To add a lovely rich flavour to the skirlie, grate in a little nutmeg and add a pinch of cinnamon towards the end.

1 Melt the butter in a pan over a medium heat and add the onion. Fry gently until it is softened and very slightly browned.

2 Stir in the rolled oats and season with salt and ground black pepper. Cook gently for 10 minutes. Taste for seasoning and serve immediately.

Per portion Energy 282kcal/1182kJ; Protein 6g; Carbohydrate 34.9g, of which sugars 2.2g; Fat 14.2g, of which saturates 6.5g; Cholesterol 27mg; Calcium 36mg; Fibre 3.5g; Sodium 91mg.

Kailkenny

This is another mashed potato combination dish, originating from the north-east of Scotland. Normally the cabbage is boiled but it is more nutritious to quickly fry it, keeping in the goodness. Kailkenny makes an excellent accompaniment to any meat dish.

Serves 4

450g/1lb potatoes, peeled and chopped

50g/2oz/¼ cup butter

50ml/2fl oz/¼ cup milk

450g/1lb cabbage, washed and finely shredded

30ml/2 tbsp olive oil

50ml/2fl oz/¼ cup double (heavy) cream

salt and ground black pepper

1 Place the potatoes in boiling water and boil for 15–20 minutes. Drain, replace on the heat for a few minutes then mash. Heat the butter and milk in a small pan and then mix into the mashed potatoes. Season to taste.

2 Heat the olive oil in a large frying pan, add the shredded cabbage and fry for a few minutes. Season to taste with salt and ground black pepper. Add the mashed potato, mix well then stir in the cream. Serve immediately.

Per portion Energy 183kcal/766kJ; Protein 3.9g; Carbohydrate 24g, of which sugars 7.3g; Fat 8.5g, of which saturates 2.4g; Cholesterol 7mg; Calcium 73mg; Fibre 3.5g; Sodium 24mg.

Spiced asparagus kale

Kale is a very important part of Scottish tradition. 'Kailyards' was the word used to describe the kitchen garden, and even the midday meal was often referred to as 'kail'. Use the more widely available curly kale if you find it hard to get the asparagus variety.

Serves 4

175g/6oz asparagus kale

10ml/2 tsp butter

25g/1oz piece fresh root ginger

15ml/1 tbsp soy sauce

salt and ground black pepper

1 Prepare the kale by removing the centre stalk and ripping the leaves into smallish pieces.

2 Heat a pan over a high heat and add the butter. As it melts, quickly add the kale and toss rapidly to allow the heat to cook it.

3 Grate the ginger into the pan and stir in thoroughly. Then add the soy sauce and mix well. When the kale has wilted, it is ready to serve.

Per portion Energy 35kcal/145kJ; Protein 1.6g; Carbohydrate 0.9g, of which sugars 0.9g; Fat 2.8g, of which saturates 1.4g; Cholesterol 5mg; Calcium 58mg; Fibre 1.4g; Sodium 301mg.

Cabbage with bacon

Bacon, especially if smoked, makes all the difference to the flavour of the cabbage, turning it into a delicious vegetable accompaniment to serve with roast beef, chicken or even a celebration turkey. Try it with people who don't like to eat greens.

Serves 4

30ml/2 tbsp oil

1 onion, finely chopped

115g/4oz smoked bacon, finely chopped

500g/1¼lb cabbage (red, white or Savoy)

salt and ground black pepper

1 Heat the oil in a large pan over a medium heat, add the chopped onion and bacon and cook for about 7 minutes, stirring occasionally.

2 Remove any tough outer leaves and wash the cabbages. Shred them quite finely, discarding the core. Add the cabbage to the pan and season. Stir for a few minutes until the cabbage begins to lose volume.

3 Continue to cook the cabbage, stirring frequently, for 8–10 minutes until it is tender but still crisp. (If you prefer softer cabbage, then cover the pan for part of the cooking time.) Serve immediately.

Variations
• This dish is equally delicious if you use spring greens (collards) instead of cabbage. You could also use curly kale.
• To make a more substantial dish to serve for lunch or supper, add more bacon, some chopped button (white) mushrooms and skinned, seeded and chopped tomatoes.

Per portion Energy 151kcal/623kJ; Protein 6.7g; Carbohydrate 7.4g, of which sugars 7g; Fat 10.5g, of which saturates 2.6g; Cholesterol 15mg; Calcium 67mg; Fibre 2.8g; Sodium 452mg.

Young vegetables with tarragon

This is almost a salad, but the vegetables here are just lightly cooked to bring out their different flavours. The tarragon adds a wonderful depth to this bright, fresh dish. It goes well as a light accompaniment to fish and seafood dishes.

Serves 4

5 spring onions (scallions)

50g/2oz/¼ cup butter

1 garlic clove, crushed

115g/4oz asparagus tips

115g/4oz mangetouts (snowpeas), trimmed

115g/4oz broad (fava) beans

2 Little Gem (Bibb) lettuces

5ml/1 tsp finely chopped fresh tarragon

salt and ground black pepper

1 Cut the spring onions into quarters lengthways and fry gently over a medium-low heat in half the butter with the garlic.

2 Add the asparagus tips, mangetouts and broad beans. Mix in, covering all the pieces with oil.

3 Just cover the base of the pan with water, season, and allow to simmer gently for a few minutes.

4 Cut the lettuce into quarters and add to the pan. Cook for 3 minutes then, off the heat, swirl in the remaining butter and the tarragon, and serve.

Per portion Energy 149kcal/619kJ; Protein 4.7g; Carbohydrate 6.1g, of which sugars 3g; Fat 12g, of which saturates 7.3g; Cholesterol 29mg; Calcium 55mg; Fibre 3.5g; Sodium 89mg.

Creamed leeks

This dish is a real Scottish favourite, delicious with a full roast dinner, or even on its own. It is very important to have good firm leeks without a core in the middle. The Scottish Musselburgh variety is excellent, if you can find it.

Serves 4

2 Musselburgh leeks, tops trimmed and roots removed

50g/2oz/½ stick butter

200ml/7fl oz/scant 1 cup double (heavy) cream

salt and ground black pepper

Cook's Tip
When buying leeks, choose smaller and less bendy ones as they are more tender.

1 Split the leeks down the middle then cut across so you make pieces approximately 2cm/¾in square. Wash thoroughly and drain in a colander.

2 Melt the butter in a large pan and when quite hot throw in the leeks, stirring to coat them in the butter, and heat through. They will wilt but should not exude water. Keep the heat high but don't allow them to colour. You need to create a balance between keeping the temperature high so the water steams out of the vegetable, keeping it bright green, whilst not burning the leeks.

3 Keeping the heat high, pour in the cream, mix in thoroughly and allow to bubble and reduce. Season with salt and ground black pepper. When the texture is smooth, thick and creamy the leeks are ready to serve.

Variation
Although these leeks have a wonderful taste themselves, you may like to add extra flavourings, such as a little chopped garlic or some chopped fresh tarragon or thyme.

Per portion Energy 363kcal/1496kJ; Protein 2.5g; Carbohydrate 3.8g, of which sugars 3.1g; Fat 37.6g, of which saturates 23.3g; Cholesterol 95mg; Calcium 51mg; Fibre 2.2g; Sodium 89mg.

Baked tomatoes with mint

This is a dish for the height of the summer when the tomatoes are falling off the vines and are very ripe, juicy and full of flavour. Mint flourishes in Lowland gardens and can also be nurtured in the Highlands. This tomato dish goes especially well with lamb.

Serves 4

6 large ripe tomatoes

300ml/½ pint/1¼ cups double (heavy) cream

2 sprigs of fresh mint

olive oil, for brushing

a few pinches of caster (superfine) sugar

30ml/2 tbsp grated Bonnet cheese

salt and ground black pepper

1 Preheat the oven to 220°C/425°F/ Gas 7. Bring a pan of water to the boil and have a bowl of iced water ready. Cut the cores out of the tomatoes and make a cross at the base. Plunge the tomatoes into the boiling water for 10 seconds and then straight into the iced water. Leave to cool completely.

2 Put the cream and mint in a pan and bring to the boil. Reduce the heat and allow to simmer until it has reduced by about half.

3 Peel the cooled tomatoes and slice them thinly.

Cook's Tip
Bonnet is a hard goat's cheese but any hard, well-flavoured cheese will do.

4 Brush a shallow gratin dish lightly with a little olive oil. Layer the sliced tomatoes in the dish, overlapping slightly, and season with salt and ground black pepper. Sprinkle a little sugar over the top.

5 Strain the reduced cream evenly over the top of the tomatoes. Sprinkle on the cheese and bake in the preheated oven for 15 minutes, or until the top is browned and bubbling. Serve immediately in the gratin dish.

Per portion Energy 443kcal/1831kJ; Protein 5g; Carbohydrate 6.7g, of which sugars 6.7g; Fat 44.1g, of which saturates 27.4g; Cholesterol 113mg; Calcium 123mg; Fibre 1.8g; Sodium 105mg.

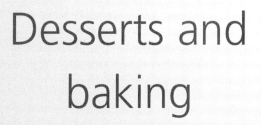

Desserts and baking

The Scots are well known for their sweet tooth, and there are plenty of delicious traditional desserts to choose from. A recurring theme is fresh berries – especially raspberries – baked in tarts, crumbles and pies or blended with creams and other dairy products. These tasty morsels are available to all to pick wild from the woodlands and hedgerows. The creams and yogurts are a speciality of the Lowlands, although throughout much of Scotland many households would have made their own.

Dunfillan bramble pudding

This warming pudding comes from Dunfillan in Perthshire. It is easy to make, if you have a little time, and is perfect with fresh cream as a tasty dessert or teatime indulgence.

Serves 4

For the Dunfillan pastry

50g/2oz/¼ cup butter

50g/2oz/¼ cup caster (superfine) sugar

1 large egg, well beaten

115g/4oz/1 cup plain (all-purpose) flour, sifted

pinch of baking powder

30ml/2 tbsp milk

grated rind of 2 lemons

For the filling

450g/1lb/4 cups blackberries

75g/3oz/scant ½ cup caster (superfine) sugar

squeeze of lemon juice

sprinkling of cornflour (cornstarch)

1 Preheat the oven to 180°C/350°F/ Gas 4. Put the blackberries in a pan and barely cover with water, then add the sugar and lemon juice. Cook until soft, about 5 minutes.

2 Transfer the blackberries to an ovenproof dish in layers, sprinkling each layer with a little cornflour.

3 To make the pastry, cream the butter and sugar then add the beaten egg. Mix the flour and baking powder then add it alternately with the milk to the butter mixture, mixing well after each addition. Finally stir in the lemon rind.

4 Spread the pastry mixture evenly over the fruit, taking small batches from the bowl and spreading carefully. Cook in the preheated oven for 20–30 minutes, or until the top is golden brown. Serve hot or cold.

Per portion Energy 366kcal/1539kJ; Protein 6.2g; Carbohydrate 60.2g, of which sugars 39.2g; Fat 12.8g, of which saturates 7.2g; Cholesterol 90mg; Calcium 122mg; Fibre 4.4g; Sodium 107mg.

Rhubarb frushie

A frushie is the old Scots word for a crumble. In this instance the topping is made with coarse rolled oats. Other fruits can be used according to preference and availability.

Serves 4

450g/1lb rhubarb or other fruit

50g/2oz/¼ cup caster (superfine) sugar or 30ml/2 tbsp redcurrant jelly

45–60ml/3–4 tbsp water

squeeze of lemon juice

For the crumble

50g/2oz/½ cup plain (all-purpose) flour

25g/1oz/scant ⅓ cup coarse rolled oats

50g/2oz/¼ cup soft light brown sugar

50g/2oz/¼ cup butter, softened

3 Combine all the ingredients for the crumble with your fingers until the mixture has a crumb-like texture.

4 Sprinkle the crumble topping evenly over the fruit. Bake for 20 minutes, until the top is crunchy and golden.

1 Preheat the oven to 200°C/400°F/ Gas 6. Cook the rhubarb or other fruit with the sugar or redcurrant jelly, water and lemon juice until soft but not mushy.

2 Transfer the cooked fruit to a deep pie dish.

Per portion Energy 267kcal/1126kJ; Protein 3.2g; Carbohydrate 41.4g, of which sugars 27.3g; Fat 11.1g, of which saturates 6.5g; Cholesterol 27mg; Calcium 141mg; Fibre 2.4g; Sodium 83mg.

Scone and butter pudding

The word scone originated in 16th-century Scotland. Scones are extremely easy to make but when you're short of time you can usually buy them from a bakery.

Serves 4

50g/2oz/scant ½ cup sultanas (golden raisins)

50g/2oz/¼ cup dried apricots, cut into small pieces

50ml/2fl oz/¼ cup whisky

300ml/½ pint/1¼ cups milk

300ml/½ pint/1¼ cups double (heavy) cream

5 egg yolks

50g/2oz/¼ cup caster (superfine) sugar

2 drops vanilla extract

6 scones

75g/3oz/6 tbsp butter

60ml/4 tbsp apricot jam, warmed

1 Place the sultanas, dried apricots and whisky in a small bowl, cover and leave to soak overnight or for at least 2 hours. At the end of the soaking time, preheat the oven to 200°C/400°F/ Gas 6.

Cook's Tip
A bain-marie is a water bath used for cooking delicate dishes, such as custards. Place the ramekin dishes in a large, shallow pan of hot water before putting in the oven.

2 Whisk the milk, cream, egg yolks, sugar and vanilla extract. Slice the tops off the scones and then slice each into three rounds. Butter each round and then layer with the fruit and custard in buttered ramekins. Set aside for 1 hour.

3 Bake in a bain-marie (see Cook's Tip) in the preheated oven for 40 minutes until risen slightly and golden-brown in colour.

4 Remove from the oven and brush with the warmed apricot jam. Serve immediately in the ramekins, or carefully pass a small sharp knife around the inside of each and gently ease the puddings out into bowls or on to individual plates.

Variation
If you prefer, you can use Drambuie or brandy in place of the whisky.

Per portion Energy 796kcal/3305kJ; Protein 8.1g; Carbohydrate 43.2g, of which sugars 43.2g; Fat 63.9g, of which saturates 37.6g; Cholesterol 399mg; Calcium 178mg; Fibre 0.5g; Sodium 187mg.

Clootie dumpling

A rich, dense pudding, traditionally made in a 'cloot', a cloth, then boiled in water over the fire. Clootie dumplings are traditionally made for the festive season.

Serves 8

225g/8oz/2 cups plain (all-purpose) flour, plus 15ml/1 tbsp for the cloot

115g/4oz/scant 1 cup suet (US chilled, grated shortening)

115g/4oz/generous 1 cup rolled oats

75g/3oz/scant ½ cup caster (superfine) sugar

5ml/1 tsp baking powder

225g/8oz/generous 1½ cups mixed sultanas (golden raisins) and currants

5ml/1 tsp each ground cinnamon and ground ginger

15ml/1 tbsp golden (light corn) syrup

2 eggs, lightly beaten

45–60ml/3–4 tbsp milk

1 Sift the flour into a dry bowl then add the suet to the flour. Using your fingertips, rub the fat into the flour until it is the texture of breadcrumbs.

2 Add the rolled oats, sugar, baking powder, fruit and spices. Mix in well then add the syrup and eggs. Stir thoroughly, using enough milk to form a firm batter.

If using an ovenproof bowl
3 Lightly grease the inside of the bowl and put the mixture in, allowing at least 2.5cm/1in space at the top. Cover with baking parchment and tie down well.

4 Put an inverted plate or saucer in the base of a deep pan, place the dumpling on top and cover with boiling water. Cook the dumpling for 2½–3 hours over a low heat.

If using a cloot
3 The cloot, or cloth, should be cotton or linen, about 52cm/21in square. Plunge it into boiling water, wring it out and lay it out on a flat surface.

4 Sprinkle 15ml/1 tbsp flour evenly over the cloot, then place the pudding mixture in the middle. Bring the corners of the cloth into the middle above the mixture and tie them with a piece of strong string, leaving space for the pudding to expand.

5 Either place the dumpling in a bain-marie (a roasting pan filled with water and placed in the oven) or steam it over a double boiler. Cook over a low heat for 2½–3 hours.

6 When the dumpling is cooked, turn it out on to a large warmed plate. Serve it in slices with hot jam and cream. It can also be eaten cold and will keep in an airtight container for a month.

Per portion Energy 902kcal/3798kJ; Protein 15.1g; Carbohydrate 143.3g, of which sugars 69.2g; Fat 35g, of which saturates 16.6g; Cholesterol 121mg; Calcium 183mg; Fibre 5.5g; Sodium 81mg.

Border tart

The Borders are particularly associated with sweet tarts that make tasty mid-morning snacks, as well as satisfying desserts. This one is delicious served hot or cold with cream.

Serves 4

250g/9oz sweet pastry (see Auld Alliance Apple Tart)

1 egg

75g/3oz/scant ½ cup soft light brown sugar

50g/2oz/¼ cup butter, melted

10ml/2 tsp white wine vinegar

115g/4oz/½ cup currants

25g/1oz/¼ cup chopped walnuts

double (heavy) cream, to serve (optional)

1 Line a 20cm/8in flan tin (tart pan) with sweet pastry. Preheat the oven to 190°C/375°F/Gas 5. Mix the egg, sugar and melted butter together.

2 Stir the vinegar, currants and walnuts into the egg mixture.

3 Pour the mixture into the pastry case and bake in the preheated oven for 30 minutes. Remove from the oven when thoroughly cooked, take out of the flan tin and leave to cool on a wire rack for at least 30 minutes. Serve on its own or with a dollop of fresh cream.

Per portion Energy 312kcal/1307kJ; Protein 3.4g; Carbohydrate 41.1g, of which sugars 41g; Fat 16.1g, of which saturates 7.3g; Cholesterol 74mg; Calcium 54mg; Fibre 0.8g; Sodium 99mg.

Auld Alliance apple tart

The Auld Alliance is a friendship that has existed between France and Scotland for some 600 years. The two countries also shared ideas on food, exemplified in this classic French dish.

Serves 4

200g/7oz/1¾ sticks butter

200g/7oz/1 cup caster (superfine) sugar

6 large eating apples

For the sweet pastry

150g/5oz/10 tbsp butter

50g/2oz/¼ cup caster (superfine) sugar

225g/8oz/2 cups plain (all-purpose) flour

1 egg

1 Make the sweet pastry. Cream the butter and sugar in a food processor. Add the flour and egg. Mix until combined, but do not to overprocess. Leave to rest in a cool place for an hour.

2 Preheat the oven to 200°C/400°F/ Gas 6. Make the filling. Cut the butter into small pieces. Using a shallow, 30cm/12in ovenproof frying pan, heat the sugar and butter and allow to caramelize over a low heat, stirring gently continuously. This will take about 10 minutes.

3 Meanwhile peel and core the apples then cut them into eighths.

4 When the butter and sugar are caramelized, place the apples in the pan in a circular fan, one layer around the outside then one in the centre. The pan should be full. Reduce the heat and cook the apples for 5 minutes then remove from heat.

5 Roll out the pastry to a circle big enough to fit the pan completely with generous edgings.

6 Spread the pastry over the fruit and tuck in the edges. Bake in the oven for about 30 minutes, or until the pastry is browned and set.

7 When cooked remove the tart from the oven and leave to rest.

8 When ready to serve, gently reheat on the stove for a few minutes then invert on to a warmed serving plate, with the pastry on the base and the apples caramelized on the top.

Per portion Energy 904kcal/3774kJ; Protein 4.6g; Carbohydrate 95.2g, of which sugars 66.5g; Fat 58.8g, of which saturates 31.5g; Cholesterol 116mg; Calcium 95mg; Fibre 3.6g; Sodium 559mg.

Whisky mac cream

The warming tipple whisky mac is a combination of whisky and ginger wine. This recipe
turns the drink into a rich, smooth, creamy dessert – very decadent.

Serves 4

4 egg yolks

15ml/1 tbsp caster (superfine) sugar,
plus 50g/2oz/¼ cup

600ml/1 pint/2½ cups double
(heavy) cream

15ml/1 tbsp whisky

green ginger wine, to serve

1 Whisk the egg yolks thoroughly
with the first, smaller amount of caster
sugar. Whisk briskly until they are
light and pale.

2 Pour the cream into a pan with the
whisky and the rest of the caster sugar.
Bring to scalding point but do not boil,
then pour on to the egg yolks, whisking
continually. Return to the pan and,
over a low heat, stir until the custard
thickens slightly.

3 Pour into individual ramekin dishes,
cover each with clear film (plastic wrap)
and leave overnight to set.

4 To serve, pour just enough green
ginger wine over the top of each
ramekin to cover the cream.

Per portion Energy 892kcal/3682kJ; Protein 5.4g; Carbohydrate 19.7g, of which sugars 19.7g; Fat 86.1g, of which saturates 51.7g; Cholesterol 407mg; Calcium 107mg; Fibre 0g; Sodium 44mg.

Malt whisky truffles

Malt whisky has long been used to flavour Scottish dishes. Here is a new speciality, blending rich chocolate with cool cream and potent whisky for a mouthwatering end to any meal.

Makes 25–30

200g/7oz dark (bittersweet) chocolate, chopped into small pieces

150ml/¼ pint/⅔ cup double (heavy) cream

45ml/3 tbsp malt whisky

115g/4oz/1 cup icing (confectioners') sugar

cocoa powder, for coating

1 Melt the chocolate in a heatproof bowl over a pan of simmering water, stirring continuously until smooth. Allow to cool slightly.

2 Using a wire whisk, whip the cream with the whisky in a bowl until thick enough to hold its shape.

Variation
You can also make Drambuie truffles by using Drambuie instead of whisky.

3 Stir in the melted chocolate and icing sugar and leave until firm enough to handle. Dust your hands with cocoa powder and shape the mixture into bite-sized balls. Coat in cocoa powder and pack into pretty cases or boxes. Store in the refrigerator for 3–4 days.

Per portion Energy 93kcal/387kJ; Protein 0.5g; Carbohydrate 10g, of which sugars 9.9g; Fat 5.5g, of which saturates 3.3g; Cholesterol 9mg; Calcium 8mg; Fibre 0.2g; Sodium 2mg.

Traditional bannock

This is a great all-purpose bread that makes an excellent breakfast with fresh butter and jams and jellies, a light lunch eaten with cheese and ham, a teatime staple toasted with butter and heather honey, or an accompaniment for dunking into thick soups and stews. The raisins add a slight sweetness with every other bite.

Makes 2 loaves

175g/6oz/generous ¾ cup soft light brown sugar

450ml/¾ pint/scant 2 cups milk

25g/1oz fresh yeast or 10ml/ 2 tsp dried

1kg/2¼lb/9 cups strong white bread flour

pinch of salt

115g/4oz/½ cup butter

115g/4oz/½ cup lard or white cooking fat

450g/1lb/generous 3 cups raisins

1 Preheat the oven to 220°C/425°F/ Gas 7. Dissolve 10ml/2 tsp of the sugar in a little of the milk for the glaze.

2 Warm a little milk, add the yeast with 5ml/1 tsp of sugar, mix to dissolve the sugar and yeast then leave to activate.

3 Put the flour with the salt in a warm place. Melt the butter and lard or white cooking fat with the remaining milk and keep warm. Mix the yeast mixture with the flour then add the milk and fat mixture. Mix together until a stiff dough forms. Knead for a few minutes, cover with a clean dish towel and leave in a warm place until it doubles in size.

4 Knock back (punch down) the dough then knead in the raisins and the remaining sugar. Shape into two rounds. Place on an oiled baking sheet, cover with a clean dish towel and leave to rise again in a warm place, until about twice the size.

5 Bake in the preheated oven for 10 minutes, then reduce the heat to 190°C/375°F/Gas 5 for about 30 minutes. Fifteen minutes before they are cooked, glaze the bannocks with the reserved milk and sugar mixture.

Per portion Energy 1924kcal/8114kJ; Protein 30.6g; Carbohydrate 330.5g, of which sugars 140g; Fat 62.5g, of which saturates 30.7g; Cholesterol 103mg; Calcium 584mg; Fibre 10g; Sodium 322mg.

Bere bannocks

Beremeal is a northern barley that grows well on Orkney, and you can still buy bannocks there made from it. If you can't get beremeal, ordinary barley flour will do instead. Bannocks were traditionally made on a girdle – a griddle – but baking them in the oven works very well. They make an excellent accompaniment to cheese.

Serves 6

225g/8oz/2 cups beremeal flour

50g/2oz/½ cup plain
(all-purpose) flour

5ml/1 tsp cream of tartar

2.5ml/½ tsp salt

5ml/1 tsp bicarbonate of soda
(baking soda)

250ml/8fl oz/1 cup buttermilk or
natural (plain) yogurt

1 Preheat the oven to 180°C/350°F/
Gas 4. Mix the beremeal flour, plain
flour, cream of tartar and salt together
in a bowl.

2 Mix the bicarbonate of soda with the buttermilk or yogurt then pour this mixture into the dry ingredients. Mix to a soft dough like a scone mix.

Variation
Bere bannocks are delicious if baked with a little cheese on top. Use a harder type of cheese, such as a good mature cheddar or Bishop Kennedy, and grate about 50g/2oz/½ cup over the surface before you put it into the oven to bake. The result is very tasty hot or cold for breakfast or lunch.

3 Turn the dough out on to a floured surface and press down with your hands to make the whole dough about 1cm/½in thick.

4 Cut the dough into six segments and place on an oiled baking sheet. Bake in the oven for about 15 minutes, or until lightly browned.

Per bannock Energy 280kcal/1192kJ; Protein 8.8g; Carbohydrate 61.4g, of which sugars 4.9g; Fat 1.8g, of which saturates 0.4g; Cholesterol 1mg; Calcium 148mg; Fibre 0.4g; Sodium 54mg.

Shortbread

The quintessential Scottish snack, shortbread is a great speciality and favourite with the Scots. It is wonderfully satisfying at any time of the day or night.

Makes about 48 fingers

oil, for greasing

275g/10oz/2½ cups plain (all-purpose) flour

25g/1oz/¼ cup ground almonds

225g/8oz/1 cup butter, softened

75g/3oz/scant ½ cup caster (superfine) sugar

grated rind of ½ lemon

1 Preheat the oven to 180°C/350°F/ Gas 4 and oil a large Swiss roll tin (jelly roll pan) or baking tray.

2 Put the remaining ingredients into a blender or food processor and pulse until the mixture comes together.

3 Place the mixture on the oiled tray and flatten it out with a palette knife or metal spatula until evenly spread. Bake in the preheated oven for 20 minutes, or until pale golden brown.

Variation
You can replace the lemon rind with the grated rind of two oranges for a tangy orange flavour, if you prefer.

4 Remove from the oven and immediately mark the shortbread into fingers or squares while the mixture is soft. Allow to cool a little, and then transfer to a wire rack and leave until cold. If stored in an airtight container, the shortbread should keep for up to two weeks.

Cook's Tip
To make by hand, sift the flour and almonds on to a pastry board or work surface. Cream together the butter and sugar in a mixing bowl and then turn the creamed mixture on to the pastry board with the flour and almonds. Work the mixture together using your fingertips. It should come together to make a smooth dough. Continue as above from Step 3.

Per finger Energy 64kcal/266kJ; Protein 0.7g; Carbohydrate 6.1g, of which sugars 1.8g; Fat 4.2g, of which saturates 2.5g; Cholesterol 10mg; Calcium 11mg; Fibre 0.2g; Sodium 29mg.

Drop scones

Variously known as girdlecakes, griddlecakes and Scotch pancakes, these make a quick and easy breakfast, elevensies or teatime a snack served with butter and drizzled with honey.

Makes 8–10

115g/4oz/1 cup plain
(all-purpose) flour

5ml/1 tsp bicarbonate of soda
(baking soda)

5ml/1 tsp cream of tartar

25g/1oz/2 tbsp butter, diced

1 egg, beaten

about 150ml/¼ pint/⅔ cup milk

a knob (pat) of butter and heather
honey, to serve

1 Lightly grease a griddle pan or heavy frying pan, then preheat it. Sift the flour, bicarbonate of soda and cream of tartar together into a mixing bowl. Add the diced butter and rub it into the flour with your fingertips until the mixture resembles fine, evenly textured breadcrumbs.

2 Make a well in the centre of the flour mixture, then stir in the egg. Add the milk a little at a time, stirring it in to check consistency. Add enough milk to give a lovely thick creamy consistency.

Cook's Tip
Placing the cooked scones in a clean folded dish towel keeps them soft and moist. Bring to the table like this and ask your guests to pull them out.

3 Cook in batches. Drop 3 or 4 evenly sized spoonfuls of the mixture, spaced slightly apart, on the griddle or frying pan. Cook over a medium heat for 2–3 minutes, until bubbles rise to the surface and burst.

4 Turn the scones over and cook for a further 2–3 minutes, until golden underneath. Place the cooked scones between the folds of a clean dish towel while cooking the remaining batter. Serve warm, with butter and honey.

Per portion Energy 90kcal/379kJ; Protein 2.8g; Carbohydrate 12.1g, of which sugars 1.1g; Fat 3.8g, of which saturates 2.1g; Cholesterol 32mg; Calcium 47mg; Fibre 0.5g; Sodium 36mg.

Black bun

This is a very traditional Scottish sweetmeat, eaten with a nip or two of whisky at the Hogmanay New Year festivities, and often given to visitors on New Year's Day. It is different from most fruit cakes because it is baked in a pastry case. It should be made several weeks in advance to give it time to mature properly.

Makes 1 cake

For the pastry

225g/8oz/2 cups plain (all-purpose) flour

115g/4oz/½ cup butter

5ml/1 tsp baking powder

cold water

For the filling

500g/1¼lb/4 cups raisins

675g/1½lb/3 cups currants

115g/4oz/1 cup chopped almonds

175g/6oz/1½ cups plain (all-purpose) flour

115g/4oz/generous ½ cup soft light brown sugar

5ml/1 tsp ground allspice

2.5ml/½ tsp each ground ginger, ground cinnamon and ground black pepper

2.5ml/½ tsp baking powder

5ml/1 tsp cream of tartar

15ml/1 tbsp brandy

1 egg, beaten, plus extra for glazing

about 75ml/5 tbsp milk

1 First make the pastry. Sift the plain flour into a mixing bowl. Remove the butter from the refrigerator ahead of time and dice it into small cubes. Leave it out of the refrigerator to soften well.

2 Add the cubes of butter to the flour. Rub the butter into the flour with your fingertips until it is the consistency of breadcrumbs. Add the baking powder and mix well. Then add small amounts of cold water, blending it in with a fork, until you can handle the mixture and knead it into a stiff dough.

3 On a floured surface, roll out the dough to a thin sheet. Grease a 20cm/8in loaf tin (pan) and line with the thin sheet of dough. Leave enough to cover the top of the cake.

4 Preheat the oven to 110°C/225°F/ Gas ¼. For the filling, put all the dry ingredients together in a dry warm bowl, including the ground spices and cream of tartar. Mix them together with a spoon until they are thoroughly blended.

5 Stir the brandy and egg into the dry filling mixture and add enough milk to moisten the mixture.

6 Put the filling into the prepared tin and cover with the remaining pastry.

7 Prick all over with a fork and brush with egg. Bake in the preheated oven for about 3 hours. Remove from the oven and leave to cool on a wire rack. Store in an airtight container.

Per cake Energy 1752kcal/7403kJ; Protein 25.8g; Carbohydrate 323.7g, of which sugars 241.9g; Fat 47.4g, of which saturates 18.5g; Cholesterol 115mg; Calcium 496mg; Fibre 11.4g; Sodium 324mg.

Tea loaf

It is always good to have a cake in the home, and fruit cakes are something of a tradition
in Scotland. This is a simple fruit cake made by soaking dried fruits in cold tea.

Makes 1 cake

450g/1lb/2⅔ cups mixed dried fruit

250g/9oz/generous 1 cup soft light
brown sugar

200ml/7fl oz/scant 1 cup cold tea

400g/1lb/4 cups self-raising (self-
rising) flour

5ml/1 tsp mixed (apple pie) spice

1 egg, beaten

1 Mix the dried fruit and sugar
together, pour the cold tea over and
leave to soak overnight.

2 The next day, preheat the oven to
190°C/375°F/Gas 5. Line a loaf tin (pan)
with baking parchment. Add the flour
and spice to the soaked fruit, stirring to
combine well, then add the beaten egg
and mix thoroughly.

3 Put the cake mixture in the prepared
loaf tin and bake in the preheated oven
for 45–50 minutes. Test with a skewer,
which should come out clean. If there is
any cake mixture sticking to the skewer,
return the cake to the oven for a few
more minutes.

Variation
For something a little more special, add
10ml/2 tsp whisky to the tea to give
the loaf an aromatic and sumptuous
flavour. Add more if you want a really
strong flavour – some people replace
the tea entirely with whisky blended
with a little water.

Per portion Energy 1012kcal/4316kJ; Protein 15.9g; Carbohydrate 245g, of which sugars 152.1g; Fat 3.4g, of which saturates 0.6g; Cholesterol 48mg; Calcium 569mg; Fibre 6.6g; Sodium 531mg.

Glamis walnut and date cake

This is a wonderfully rich and moist cake perfect for afternoon tea. The dates are first soaked before being added to the cake mixture. This gives the cake a lovely texture.

Makes 1 cake

225g/8oz/1⅓ cups chopped dates

250ml/8fl oz/1 cup boiling water

5ml/1 tsp bicarbonate of soda (baking soda)

225g/8oz/generous 1 cup caster (superfine) sugar

1 egg, beaten

275g/10oz/2¼ cups plain (all-purpose) flour

2.5ml/½ tsp salt

75g/3oz/6 tbsp butter, softened

5ml/1 tsp vanilla extract

5ml/1 tsp baking powder

50g/2oz/½ cup chopped walnuts

1 Put the chopped dates into a warm, dry bowl and pour the boiling water over the top; it should just cover the dates. Add the bicarbonate of soda and mix in thoroughly. Leave to stand for 5–10 minutes.

2 Preheat the oven to 180°C/350°F/ Gas 4. Lightly grease a 23 x 30cm/ 9 x 12in cake tin (pan) and line with baking parchment.

3 In a separate mixing bowl, combine all the remaining ingredients for the cake. Then mix in the dates, along with the soaking water until you have a thick batter. You may find it necessary to add a little more boiling water to help the consistency.

4 Pour or spoon the batter into the tin and bake in the oven for 45 minutes. Cut into thick wedges when cool.

Per portion Energy 749kcal/3155kJ; Protein 10.5g; Carbohydrate 125.5g, of which sugars 77.8g; Fat 26.2g, of which saturates 11g; Cholesterol 88mg; Calcium 153mg; Fibre 3.4g; Sodium 141mg.

Index